"*Legacy* is suffused with reverence for the Constitution...."

Kenneth S. Lynn
The Washington Post Book World

"An unusual book... Themes that have concerned Michener in other books—democracy, freedom, religious tolerance, women's suffrage... {are} deftly and thoughtfully handled in the familiar... Michener manner."

Edward Rutherfurd
Chicago Tribune

"A highly personal view of the history of America... Packed with fascinating detail. That the writing is good goes without saying."

Associated Press

"The political commentary stitched into *Legacy* comes from a writer who has been assessing the national agenda for as long as he's controlled a forum."

Carlin Romano
The Philadelphia Inquirer

Also by James Michener:

FICTION

TALES OF THE SOUTH PACIFIC*
RETURN TO PARADISE*
THE BRIDGES AT TOKO-RI*
SAYONARA*
SELECTED WRITINGS
THE FIRES OF SPRING*
HAWAII*
CARAVANS*
THE SOURCE*
THE DRIFTERS*
CENTENNIAL*
CHESAPEAKE*
THE WATERMEN
THE COVENANT*
SPACE*
POLAND*
TEXAS*
ALASKA

NONFICTION

THE BRIDGE AT ANDAU*
RASCALS IN PARADISE*
JAPANESE PRINTS: FROM EARLY MASTERS TO
    THE MODERN
IBERIA: SPANISH TRAVELS AND REFLECTIONS*
MODERN JAPANESE PRINT: AN APPRECIATION
PRESIDENTIAL LOTTERY: THE RECKLESS GAM-
    BLE IN OUR ELECTORAL SYSTEM
SPORTS IN AMERICA*
KENT STATE: WHAT HAPPENED AND WHY*
THE FLOATING WORLD

*Published by Fawcett Books

LEGACY

James A. Michener

FAWCETT CREST • NEW YORK

Contents

The Starrs

MY BAD LUCK started just before Christmas 1985. But at the time, as so often happens, it seemed like good luck.

I had graduated from West Point just in time to join the final fighting in the rice paddies of Vietnam. Returning with a chest full of medals, a few earned, most routine, I married Nancy Makin, a girl from Maryland whom I'd been dating whenever I found myself with stateside duty. We had spent our first three years of married life in the Panama Canal Zone, where I had the shameful task of watching as Jimmy Carter gave away that marvel of engineering to the Panamanians. My father, a colonel in the Army Reserve and a noted hero in World War II, called it mildly 'the most traitorous act of any American since Aaron Burr.' And believe me, considering what Aaron Burr had done to our family as well as our nation in the early 1800s, that was a savage indictment.

It was in Panama that I mastered Spanish, which led to further assignments south of the border; and in Argentina, Chile and especially Guatemala, learning firsthand about Communist subversion on our doorstep.

I was never gung ho in my work against the Reds. That's not my style. I don't like to be out front unless war's been declared and I'm in charge of troops. But no one had greater aversion to Communism than I did, after the butchery I'd seen in Nam and the cruel behavior in Guatemala.

I've never known whether it was my familiarity with Latin American Communism or my Spanish that accounted for the unexpected promotion, but on 10 December 1985, I received orders to leave my duty station in Cartagena, Colombia, where we were trying to stanch the flow of cocaine into the States, and report to the Pentagon.

Nancy rejoiced at what she called 'a long-overdue assignment,' not only because it meant a promotion, which I needed if I was ever going to make colonel, but also because it allowed me to rejoin her in Washington, where she had established our permanent home. I appreciated the new job because I would be working with men who had been in my class at the Point or on duty with me in Nam.

My duties were well matched to my experience: liaison with the various military commissions from South and Central American nations, anti-Communism in general, and exciting duty with Vice-President Bush's special task force on drug smuggling. I met Bush only a couple of times, always in a crowd of officers, but from my earliest days in Colombia, I'd had a favorable opinion of what he was trying to do.

And then, just before Christmas, I was suddenly handed the exciting news: 'Starr, an opportunity like this doesn't reach down to tap a major very often. Your Spanish and all, or maybe it's your strong record in Guatemala. Anyway, they want you for a stint at the National Security Council.'

'Am I qualified?'

'The Army wants you to go. Demands that you go. Too damned many Navy and Marine types over there.'

'My duties?'

'Cloak-and-dagger? Who ever knows?' He was a two-star general, and he half saluted before I did: 'Keep your nose clean this time, Starr. We want you back. Men like you are too precious to lose.'

His last words spoiled the good news, because they reminded both him and me that my promotion to lieutenant colonel had been sidetracked. Normally, an Army officer, if he's good, expects regular promotion up to the rank of lieutenant colonel. The real weeding out occurs in the jump from light-chicken to full-chicken. As my West Point bunkmate Zack McMaster once said in his poetic way: 'Any asshole can make light colonel. It takes a real man to handle the next leap.' He had left the service after only two years, for it had become clear that because of his outspoken manner, he would never hack it.

My promotion had been held up twice because of an incident in Chile. Information I was picking up on the street, where I moved about in civilian clothes, led me to believe that one of our clandestine exercises was bound to backfire, allowing a gang of real murderers to sneak behind the American flag while they continued their dirty games. I protested in an embassy meeting, failed to get attention, and sat down to write a forceful memorandum. My grandfather, having undergone two messy divorces in which his ardent letters betrayed him, had summarized his experience in a pithy command: 'Do right and fear no man. Don't write and fear no woman.' Forgetting half of this, I drafted a memo that turned out to make my superiors look bad. Infuriated, they had blocked my advancement.

Zack, who had turned to law after his nonproductive fling with the Army, had enrolled at Columbia Law, graduated high, served as clerk to Justice Byron White of the Supreme Court, and gone on to become one of Washington's street-smart geniuses who know where the bodies are buried. But if he did a lot of manipulating, he also did much *pro bono* work. When my promotion was blocked by the bad vibes from Chile, he advised me: 'Starr, if you move to another command, keep a low profile and do a superior job. Then not even your enemies will be able to hold you back.' My assignment to the NSC proved him right.

But his urgent phone call this morning put an end to that strategy: 'Starr, old buddy. You're in serious trouble.'

'How do you know?'

'A Washington lawyer is supposed to know everything.'

'Like what?'

'The Senate Committee on the Iran deal wants to interrogate you. You'll be notified today.'

'Zack, I've had nothing to do with Iran.'

'The angle isn't Iran. It's the contras.'

Suddenly my mouth went dry, for the contra affair was much different from the Iranian, and this time I could not paint myself as lily-white. There was, after all, the Tres Toros affair about which rumors had begun to circulate, and I would not feel easy being interrogated about that. 'You better come on over.'

'Wouldn't it be better if I stayed away from the White House? Your home maybe?'

Today, twenty-four hours later, I can recall every thought that assailed me in the fifteen minutes it took Zack and me, by different routes, to reach our condo in Georgetown. First I clarified my mind as to Iran:

Did the Iran project touch me in any way? Never. I knew vaguely that something was under way—but details? I never had a clear word from anyone. How about Lieutenant Colonel Oliver North, did I really know him? I heard from everyone that he was a fine dedicated patriot, but I never had direct contact with him on anything to do with Iran. On Iran, I am squeaky clean.

But how about Nicaragua? Now, there I did bump into North a couple of times. Strictly professional, strictly within the law, so far as I know. I reported to him twice on the effectiveness of the contra effort. Tried to brief him on the bad cocaine situation in Colombia, but he was too occupied with other things. Did I ever receive orders from him? Never. Did I ever propose Central American actions to him? Never.

But if I wasn't on Colonel North's team, and I wasn't, what in hell was I doing in Central America from Christmas '85 to Christmas '86? I'm so damned security-conscious that I won't even spell out in these notes the gory details. All I'll say is that even at Tres Toros, my actions were inspired by patriotism, my conviction that Communism is a deadly peril, and my belief that the free world must not sit back and let the Reds run rampant. But if I knew nothing about Iran, I did know a great deal about Nicaragua, and I approved ninety-five percent of what we were doing down there. And then, as I approached the street leading to our house, my stomach turned to ice, and I found myself saying aloud, as if my wife were sitting next to me: 'This is not going to be easy.'

When I entered our house I was relieved to see that Nancy wasn't home. Explaining complex things to her is never easy, because she has the habit of interrupting with questions that probe embarrassing alleyways.

When Zack arrived, it was as if we were back at the Point. He even wore his three-piece suit with the trim appearance of a uniform, and like always, he seemed to keep four steps ahead of me. I was glad to have him on my side.

After clearing a place on our table for his papers and yellow note pad, he said: 'Let's get right down to cases. Do you consider yourself guilty of anything?'

'Like what? Traffic violations?'

He looked at me almost with contempt, and in a harsh, unfamiliar voice said: 'I mean this Iran mess.'

'Never touched Iran even remotely.'

'You can swear to that?'

'I just said so, didn't I?'

Zack pushed himself away from the table, took a hard look at me, and said: 'Look here, soldier. You could be in deep mud, and to save your neck I need to know the absolute truth. You know how men like you stumble into fatal error? Lying under oath. The Feds double back ten years later, confront you with your earlier perjured testimony, and throw you in the slammer. Tomorrow, before the Senate Committee you'll take an oath, so I'm going to question you today as if you just had. And if you lie, you go to prison . . . for a long, long term.'

I am amazed at what I said next, but it was the reaction of a man who had always worked for a limited government salary: 'How much is this going to cost? Your legal fee, I mean?'

'Starr! My firm is doing this for free. Because I know you're honest.' He stopped. 'You got problems, Major. I'm here as your bunkmate.' Now he got down to business: 'I'll take your word that it wasn't Iran that got you into trouble. So it's got to be the contra connection. Tell me about your role in that beauty.'

'You're right, it must be Nicaragua. But I can't go public with much.'

'Before this is over, I assure you, you'll go very public.' And he began to bombard me with many questions, and such intimate ones that quite often I had to say: 'That one I can't answer. National security.'

Once he stormed: 'I'm your *lawyer*, dammit! I have to know.'

'Not that, you don't.'

So we agreed on a procedure that didn't please him but which we could live with. We reviewed my Army career, my near court-martial, my delayed promotion, my unceasing fights against the two enemies Communism and drugs, and my publicly acknowledged work for the Security Council in Central America. But concerning the secret operations, I would not allow myself to be questioned. This infuriated Zack: 'Dammit, Norman, I can't handle your case unless you give me short, honest answers to three questions. One, were you pretty deep in the contra affair?'

'Yes.'

'Two, did you ever do anything illegal?'

'I always had authorization.' I hesitated, a fact which he noticed, then changed my answer: 'Better make that, I always thought I had.'

'Three, could a civilian jury find you guilty of anything?'

'If the facts were presented to them with a twist, yes.'

Zack stopped. Dead-cold. Not even his motor running. He went to the window, studied the street as if afraid we were being watched, and I could see that he was trying to devise our strategy, but then he laughed in his old red-headed way and came back to me as if he were starting an entirely new conversation.

Grasping me by the shoulder, he said: 'You're in a dangerous position, old friend. The public smells blood on this contra affair and they're hungry for victims. But there may be a way out.'

'There better be. I do not fancy a prison term.'

'It's my job to see that you don't get one. If you lose, I lose, and in this town, I cannot afford to be seen as a loser.'

At this point Nancy came in through the front door. Five feet one and eighty-percent high explosive, she was lugging two big brown paper bags from the supermarket, and before she could put them down she saw Zack, ran across the room, and gave him a hearty kiss: 'What brings you here, Counselor? According to the papers, you keep a lot of irons in the fire.'

'None bigger than this one, Nancy,' he said, and he invited her to join us. 'The bloodhounds are after your old man, and it's my job to get him safely across the ice.'

'Serious?'

'Very.'

'The Iran affair?' My wife is a clever woman, always willing to make leaps in the dark.

'Worse. The contra affair. Central America.'

As I had done earlier when Zack threw those loaded words at me, she sort of choked, grew pale, and disclosed much more than I had: 'Anyone who worked closely with the contras, and Norman did, has got to be under suspicion. And since Norman . . .'

'Stop right there!' I interrupted, and Zack, looking at both of us with the familial affection he so often displayed, especially since his divorce had left him without a real home of his own, said: 'Relax, you two. Let me do the worrying.' And he left our house with a very worried look.

Jared
Starr

1726–1787

AT SIX-THIRTY Friday morning our doorbell jangled, and it was Zack: 'Couldn't sleep. Kept devising alternate strategies, came up with about eight, none outstanding.'

When Nancy joined us in her bathrobe she said: 'Join the club. We couldn't sleep, either.' And when she brought out the coffee she said, as she handed Zack his: 'You will keep us out of trouble, won't you?' and he said: 'That's my job.'

He didn't waste time on social niceties. Sitting with both hands clasped about his cup to keep them warm, he asked: 'Norman, didn't you tell me once at the Point that some of your family, I mean one or two of your ancestors way back, weren't they involved in the Army? Our national history and all that?'

'Nearly all of them.'

'Refresh me.'

I went to the bookshelf by the fireplace, took down my 1985 *World Almanac* and placed paper markers at the two pages my family was proud of, and handed it to him: 'Four forty-three, look who signed the Declaration of Independence, toward the bottom of the list, under the S's.' The print was quite small, but there after the noble name of Roger Sherman, Connecticut, came that of Jared Starr, Virginia. Major in the Continental Army, served in the final battle of the Revolution at Yorktown, 1781.

'Quite a record. He'll prove very helpful to us. Didn't you also say he signed the Constitution?'

'That was his son. Look on page four forty-seven,' and there, in minute print under the heading *Virginia*, came two names, the first more distinguished than the second: James Madison, Jr., Simon Starr. I could see that Zack was impressed, but at this point he didn't care to say so: 'Didn't you have a rather well-known general in your family, too? Civil War, maybe?'

'General Hugh Starr, always fought close to General Lee. Many battles. Attested to the surrender at

Appomattox, then lived to eighty-eight, firing Confederate fusillades all the way.'

'Anyone else we can use to keep you out of prison?'

'Well, my father won the Congressional Medal of Honor at Saipan in 1944.'

'He did? You never told me.'

'Rather simple. Marines formed the two outer flanks, Army the middle. Both generals were named Smith. "Howling Mad" the Marine was in charge, Ralph the Army man led the unlucky Twenty-seventh Division, mostly New York National Guard. Clerks and shopkeepers principally, with my father as a West Point light colonel attached to lend some professionalism.

'Divided commands are hell, as we learned at the Point. This was classic. Two conflicting doctrines. The Marines roared ahead, leaving enemy hedge-hogs behind. The Army, properly methodical, cleaned out everything, but to tell the truth, we did lag . . . Hell of a mess. Finally, "Howling Mad" relieved Ralph of command. Said the Marines would finish the job alone. Unprecedented.

'My father went ape. Later claimed he had not been told of the order to hold fast where he was and let the Marines take over. Led his men on a fantastic surge forward, performed what they called "incredible feats of valor." Lost his left leg, and earned a place in Army history for getting a court-martial on Saturday and notice of his Congressional Medal of Honor on Monday.'

Zack reflected on the history of my four military

ancestors, and said: 'You Starrs are patriots, aren't you? If we play this right, no Senate investigation can touch you.'

'But the culpability?'

'What do you mean?'

'It always seemed to me, during the various courts-martial on which I served, that there were two conditions. Legal guilt and moral culpability. They're not always the same.'

This irritated him slightly: 'Forget the legal niceties. Attending to them is my job. That's what I get paid for.' This was apparently his standard advice to clients, but this time we both laughed, because he wasn't getting paid.

'How do you plan to use this background stuff?'

'I'm not sure yet, but what I want you to do, and you can help him in this, Nancy, is review what you've just told me. Get it lead-pipe solid in your mind, because this afternoon before the Senate it just might become important, if they elect to go down those garden paths.'

When he left us at seven, we dug out some family heirlooms, old papers and pamphlets that my grandfather Richard had collected. He was proud of our family, and spent his wasted life trying to prove that the Starrs were more distinguished than the facts justified, but he did come up with a surprising batch of material.

I had barely begun refreshing myself on old Jared Starr, when the phone rang: 'Norman? Zack. Great news! I've persuaded the Senate staff to postpone your appearance till Monday morning. Do your homework.' He did not even wait for me to respond, but since the urgency in his voice made it clear that he was totally involved in my case, I felt the least I could do was follow his instructions. So before heading for the White House, I considered the case of the rambunctious founder of our clan.

Jared Starr was a gritty old fellow, seven generations back, and he would probably have made some dramatic contribution to the writing of our Constitution had he not been such an ardent patriot. He first attracted public attention in rural Virginia in 1774 when he boldly supported Patrick Henry in the agitation for freedom. Two years later, in Philadelphia, he affixed his challenging signature to the Declaration of Independence, and without returning to his farm, volunteered to serve in General Washington's ragtag army, in which he rose to the rank of major.

He fought in many hopeless battles, usually as the oldest man in his detachment, and, as he told his children in later years, 'I became a master of retreat.' In the closing months of the war he met up with someone who would lead him to what would be the outstanding experience of his life: he was seconded to a regiment in which he found himself next to a dashing West Indian immigrant, Alexander Hamilton, whom he described eventually as 'the bravest man I've ever known and the brightest.'

At the culminating Battle of Yorktown in 1781,

Starr followed Hamilton on a daring charge into British lines which helped turn the tide of this engagement. 'Had I looked behind me,' said Hamilton at the dinner celebrating the end of the Revolution, 'and not seen Jared Starr puffing along like a wearied dog at the end of a chase, I doubt I would have had the courage to enter the enemy lines.' Then, bending a pewter spoon, Hamilton fashioned a rude medal, which he stuck into a tear in Jared's blouse. 'Honors of battle,' he cried with a rare enthusiasm.

After the British surrender, Starr retired to his Virginia farm, where he watched with growing despair as the thirteen states of his new nation fumbled and stumbled their way toward chaos. But in these doom-filled days he sought guidance and reassurance from Hamilton through the series of letters the two patriots exchanged: 'Dear Colonel Hamilton, I see chaos threatening from all sides. Our Continental Congress can assess taxes on each of the thirteen states but cannot force them to pay. It can call for an army to protect us, but not conscript any soldiers from the states to serve. What can we do to save our nation?'

Hamilton's responses never varied: 'We must either put backbone into our present form of government or construct a better,' and just as Starr in his remote corner of Virginia had supported Patrick Henry in the call for freedom, he now echoed Alexander Hamilton's comparable cry for reform. In the spring of 1786 neither Hamilton nor Starr was yet brave enough to openly call for abandonment of the inept Articles of Confederation, under which the new states were trying to govern themselves, but each knew that the other was at least contemplating a radical new form of government.

In the late summer, Hamilton and a few others like him invited the thirteen states to send delegates to an informal gathering in Annapolis, Maryland, for a discussion of steps that might have to be taken if the precious American experiment in self-government was to be saved. But despite the growing anarchy, only five states bothered to respond—New York, New Jersey, Pennsylvania, Delaware, Virginia—and even they sent only twelve participants in all.

The Annapolis adventure was a failure, but Hamilton of New York and Starr of Virginia were resolute fighters who badgered the others with prophecies of doom if something was not done, so that in the end the twelve plotters mustered the courage to send a rallying cry to all the states: 'Let us convene a grand assembly in Philadelphia in the spring of next year.'

Hamilton, who could rarely abide vagueness, made a motion: 'Make it the fourteenth of May 1787,' and in a loud voice Starr cried: 'Second the motion!' and it was done. As the two friends parted, Hamilton said: 'Starr, we've work to do between now and May,' and the Virginian nodded as he turned away.

He had taken only two steps when he felt his right arm grabbed forcefully from behind. It was Hamilton and, leaning close to Starr's ear, he said: 'Jared, we either lay the groundwork for a new nation . . . or watch the old one sputter out like a spent fire.'

The solemnity of this challenge awed Starr, and for a moment he surveyed the backs of the delegates as they said their farewells. 'Colonel, I think most of these men came here honor-pledged to mend the present Articles and under no circumstances to bring in a radical substitution.'

Hamilton stood rigid: 'Do you think the miserable system we have today can be fixed? No! Neither do I.'

'Shouldn't we in decency expose our thinking now?'

'No,' Hamilton said, 'because today all would oppose us. But eight months from now, when we meet to solve the matter, all will see that our way is the only practical one.' They parted with a handshake.

On his lonely ride home from Annapolis to Virginia, his thoughts and his horse his only companions, my fighting ancestor hammered out two convictions from which no political storms could ever divert him: We've got to have a strong new government. But the rights of Virginia must be protected in whatever changes we make.

Had the times been placid, Jared would have gone home, agitated quietly among his neighbors for a new form of government, and reported to Philadelphia in May of 1787, ready to continue the bold work he had helped launch with the Declaration of Independence. He would surely have supported Hamilton in the latter's drive for a powerful central government, even though it would be marked by many of the more successful aristocratic and monarchical characteristics of British rule.

But the times were not placid. The ramshackle government by which former colonies tried to organize their Atlantic seaboard was so ridiculously inefficient that it seemed about to collapse from any one of many weaknesses: the inability to impose or collect taxes; the lack of a strong court system; a pathetic weakness in the face of likely invasions from Europe; and the absence of an effective way to settle internal arguments among the states. Since everyone who loved America recognized these weaknesses, her enemies must have seen them too.

Then, as if to illustrate in one dramatic gesture the low estate into which American government had fallen, in rural Massachusetts a rabble-rousing countryman named Daniel Shays said he could tolerate no longer the grievous hurts he and his kind suffered at the hands of the well-to-do. Seeking redress, he launched a minor revolution against the tyranny of the local courts, the banks, and most other manifestations of government.

He was forty years old that winter, an inspired agrarian so persuasive in his fiery harangues that he collected about him a substantial following of Massachusetts farmers. They demanded only simple things: a larger supply of paper money with which to pay their heavy debts; an end to courts' throwing honest men into bankruptcy and jail; and general freedom from what Shays called 'the oppressive government of the rich.'

During the cold winter of 1786–87, Shays and his wild men so terrorized western Massachusetts that his Rebellion, as it was now formally called, threatened to expand into neighboring states. A shudder passed along the Atlantic seaboard as anxious men asked: 'Is this a foretaste of destruction to come?' And those who were being designated by their various states to attend the Philadelphia meeting spent the cold months wondering: What can we do to stop this rot? George Washington wrote to John Adams, Thomas Jefferson in Paris wrote to George Mason in Virginia, and Hamilton corresponded with scores of patriots, all seeking a practical answer to the question which overrode all others: What can be done to save the nation?

No one pondered the question more than Jared Starr, for he had helped launch this experiment in self-government and did not propose to sit idly by as men unwilling to make difficult decisions allowed it to break apart and crumble. So, when disruption threatened as a result of Shays' Rebellion, he knew what he must do.

Riding north from his farm, he stopped in Philadelphia to consult with the sturdy patriots of that bustling commercial city, went on to New York to assure Hamilton that Virginia would be sending first-class men to the impending convention, and then on to Boston, where he offered his support to the government that was struggling to put down Shays' Rebellion.

'How old are you?' the colonel in charge of the local militia asked, and Starr said through clenched teeth: 'Sixty-one . . . service under Washington and Hamilton.'

'We don't need grandfathers,' the colonel said, and he would not accept Jared into the formal militia.

So Starr moved west under his own command, associated himself with an improvised force under General Benjamin Lincoln, and during a skirmish at the Springfield depot took two musket balls through his left hip.

Disgusted by his carelessness and infuriated by the brazen manner in which the revolutionaries escaped to the north, Major Starr badgered the nurses who tried to attend him and refused the doctors permission to amputate his festering left leg. When it became obvious that he was about to die, he penned a letter of instruction to his son Simon back on their Virginia farm:

> The leg don't get better. Advise Colonel Hamilton. And make plans to fill my spot at the next meeting in Philadelphia on 14 May next. Remember the two obligations we undertook. Fashion a strong new form of government but protect Virginia's interests. You can safely follow Colonel Hamilton in such matters.

Still fulminating against nurses, doctors and revolutionaries, he died at the end of March 1787, less than seven weeks before fifty-five other patriots much like himself convened to see what steps might be taken to rescue the United States from disintegration.

Simon
Starr

1759–1807

I'VE ALWAYS had difficulty explaining to my wife and my friends the curious role played by Simon Starr in the writing of the Constitution. Because he was a most excellent man and one of the founders who attended every session of the Convention, Nancy likes to imagine him standing before the members and orating with such persuasion that he modified the course of debate.

Alas, it wasn't that way, so on Friday morning

before I left for my duties in the basement of the White House, I scanned my grandfather Richard's copy of the informal notes Simon left regarding his role in the Convention, and asked her to refresh her memory while I headed for the lion's den.

By the time I reached the White House, word had circulated that I was to testify before the Senate Committee on Monday, so while Nancy spent her spare time with the Convention battles of 1787, I was immersed in the political battles of 1987.

Of course, all my military co-workers dropped by inconspicuously to wish me well, and at least three used exactly the same words: 'Hang in there, champ,' as if I were a boxer getting hell pasted out of me. I felt that way, a reaction not diminished when Zack phoned me rather breathlessly: 'Norman, can you meet me at your place? Immediately?'

'It's only eleven.'

'I said immediately,' and when I reached home he was fretting impatiently on the stoop because Nancy wasn't in. Friday was her day at the military hospital, where she read to men who had been blinded in one action or another around the world. Once inside, he asked, before sitting down: 'Soldier, do you have a decent uniform? Good, bring it out. Now, what fruit salad can we slap on it? I want everything.'

He said that since I was going to appear before the Senate as a man who might be accused of secret misbehavior, he wanted me to stand forth in what he called 'blazing patriotic glory,' which meant he wished to check my ribbons, all sixteen.

'Are these first three of personal significance?'

'They are.'

'That amazing job you did on the swamp installation in Vietnam?'

'That's the second one.'

'The first? You do something I missed?'

'The swamp was routine. Barely deserves a medal. This one was for real. Saving a corporal's life under . . . well, unusual circumstances.'

'Care to specify?'

'It was earned. President Nixon said so when he pinned it on. Jabbed right into my skin. Quite clumsy.'

Zack sat at the table for several minutes staring at my medals and arranging the four tiers in different patterns. Abruptly he asked: 'Could I see your *Almanac* again?' and when I handed it to him, he said almost brusquely: 'Find me those pages about your ancestors.'

It required only a few minutes for him to reassure himself about the Starr names, after which he spent several minutes idly scanning familiar phrases in the Declaration and the Constitution. With a bold gesture that indicated he had made up his mind, he slammed the book shut, strode to the door, and left. But from the street he called back: 'Your uniform. Get it dry-cleaned.'

On 9 May 1787, when Simon Starr left his family plantation in northern Virginia and started his five-day horseback ride to the Constitutional Convention in Philadelphia, he carried with him the letter of instruction his father had sent from his deathbed in western Massachusetts: '. . . make plans to fill my spot . . . Fashion a strong new form of government but protect Virginia's interests.' More than most delegates, Simon appreciated how difficult it would be to fulfill these two commands.

In the first place, his elders in Virginia had made it clear that he and the other delegates were authorized merely 'to correct and improve our present Articles of Confederation, and under no circumstances to meddle with any new form of government.' For him to achieve what his father had wanted, a strong central government, would require ignoring these instructions.

In the second place, he realized that a new union could not be established unless the three big states—Massachusetts in the North, with its manufacturing; Pennsylvania in the middle, with its commerce; Virginia in the South, with its tobacco and cotton plantations—found some way to protect their majority interests while ensuring the small states like Rhode Island, New Hampshire and Delaware a respectable voice in whatever form of government emerged. Up to now, it had been one state–one voice, but with the big states constantly accumulating more power and responsibility, such an imbalance could not continue. Rhode Island did not carry the weight of Virginia in population, trade or wealth, and to claim that she did was folly.

He was perplexed as to how this impasse would

be resolved, but he was sure of one thing: he would never allow Virginia's rights to be trampled.

Simon was twenty-eight years old that spring, a graduate of the College of New Jersey at Princeton, red-headed, quick to anger, interested in all aspects of American life. He had served as foot soldier in the latter years of the Revolution, rising to the rank of captain, but he had known none of the commanding figures of that period. In recent years, however, he had corresponded with two of the most brilliant men in Virginia or the nation, George Mason and George Wythe, the dazzling professor of law at William and Mary College. Simon was literate, informed, patriotic, and determined to conduct himself with distinction at the Convention.

As he left that May he assured his wife and young son: 'I'll be back for the fall harvest,' and as he rode down the long lane to the highway, he called out the same message to the slaves who lined the pathway to bid him farewell.

In his compact canvas saddle bags he carried four books he had come to treasure at college: Thucydides' account of the Greek wars, John Locke's treatise on government, a book by Adam Smith on the political economy of nations, a saucy novel by Henry Fielding. In his head he carried about as good an education as was then available in either the United States or Great Britain, but in both Princeton and Virginia he had been careful to mask any pretension to superiority. He was an earnest young man of solid ability who would always show deference to his elders. As one of the two youngest members of the Convention he would feel himself at a disadvantage, but he intended to associate himself with older men of talent and make his contribution through supporting them.

He rode into Philadelphia, a burgeoning city of some forty thousand, in the late afternoon of Sunday, 13 May 1787, and without difficulty found Market Street, the main east-west thoroughfare, which he pursued toward the Delaware River until he came to Fourth Street. Here, in accordance with instructions, he turned south till he saw ahead, swaying in the evening breeze, the reassuring signboard of the Indian Queen Tavern. He tied his horse, took down his saddle bags, and strode inside to announce himself to the innkeeper: 'Simon Starr of Virginia, for the room assigned to my father, Jared Starr.'

At the mention of this name, several men who had been idly talking showed great interest and moved forward to meet the newcomer. In the next exciting moments he met members of the Virginia delegation, including four men of distinction: Edmund Randolph, James Madison, and the two older scholars with whom he'd been in correspondence, George Mason and George Wythe. Looking carefully at each as he was introduced, he said: 'And General Washington's a Virginian, too. Add him to you gentlemen, and Virginia's to be strongly represented,' and Madison said quietly: 'We planned it that way.'

'I rode hard to get here for tomorrow's opening session,' Starr said, to which Madison replied, with a touch of asperity: 'No need. There'll be no session.'

'Why?' and young Starr learned the first basic fact about the Convention: 'Takes seven of the thirteen states to form a legal quorum. Only four are here now.'

'When will the others arrive?' and Madison said sourly: 'Who knows?'

Eleven days were wasted in idleness as delegates straggled in, and each evening Madison informed those already in attendance of the situation: 'Two more states reported today. Perhaps by the end of next week.' If the nation was, as the Virginia delegation believed, in peril, the men designated to set it right seemed in no hurry to start.

And shortly, there was sobering news: 'Rhode Island has refused to have anything to do with our Convention and will send no delegates.' This meant that only twelve states would do the work.

One night during the waiting period Starr returned to the Indian Queen, to see a group of delegates speaking with a newcomer, a slender, handsome, self-contained young man of thirty, so compelling in his manner that Simon whispered to a friend: 'Who's that?' and when the man said: 'Alexander Hamilton, just in from New York,' Starr gasped so loudly that the newcomer turned, gazed at him with penetrating eyes, and said, almost grandly: 'Yes?'

'I'm Jared Starr's son.'

And now the rather icy reserve which Hamilton had been showing melted in the sun of remembered friendship. Elbowing his way out of the crowd, he hurried to Simon, embraced him warmly with both arms, and cried: 'When I learned of your father's death I felt mortally stricken. A man rarely finds such a trusted friend.'

They spent three hours together that first night, with Hamilton probing in a dozen different directions to determine Starr's attitudes, and as the evening waned, it became clear that the two men had even more in common than Hamilton had had with old Jared Starr. Both believed in a strong kind of central government, in the right of large states to exercise large powers, and particularly in the sanctity of property. But toward the end of that first exploration Simon heard several of Hamilton's opinions which could be interpreted as an inclination toward a monarchical form of government: 'Simon, the world is divided into those with power and those without. Control of government must rest with the former, because they have most at hazard. Whatever kind of supreme ruler we devise, he should serve for life and so should the members of the stronger house, if we have more than one. That way we avoid the domination of the better class by the poorer.'

'Poorer? Do you mean money?'

Hamilton bit on his knuckle: 'Yes, I suppose I do. But I certainly want those with no money to have an interest in our government. But actually voting? No, no. That should be reserved for those with financial interests to protect.'

When Simon accompanied Hamilton to the door of the Indian Queen, he experienced a surge of devotion for this brilliant young man, so learned, so sure of himself, so clear-minded in his vision of what his adopted nation needed: 'Father told me that you were the best man he'd ever met, Colonel Hamilton. Tonight I understand why.' Then, hesitantly, he added: 'If I can help you in the days ahead, please let me know. You can depend on my support.'

In the next week, when the delegates chafed because a quorum had still not reached Philadelphia, Simon remained close to his Virginia delegation and watched with what care they laid their plans to assume intellectual and political control of the Convention. The three awesome minds, Mason, Madison and Wythe, perfected a general plan they had devised for a wholly new government, and it was agreed that at the first opportunity on opening day, the imposing Edmund Randolph would present it as a working paper around which the other delegates would have to frame their arguments. 'If we put up a good plan,' Madison said, 'we'll probably lose two-thirds of the minor details, but the solid structure will still remain.'

At the close of the Convention, a hundred and sixteen days later, Simon Starr would draft a perceptive memorandum regarding his major experiences; these notes would not record the great debates or the machinations by which the new government was formed, but they would depict honestly one young man's reactions to the men who gathered in Philadelphia that hot summer, and no entry was more illuminating than his summary of the people involved:

> Only twelve states nominated delegates and they authorized a total of 74 men to come to Philadelphia. Of these, only 55 bothered to appear for any of the sessions, and of these, only 41 stayed to the bitter end, but of these, only 39 were willing to sign our finished document.

One of his entries that was widely quoted in later years dealt with the composition of the membership, and although the comments on those who were there could have been provided by other observers, his list of those who were conspicuous by their absence was startling:

> I was surprised at how many delegates had college degrees like my own. Harvard, Yale, King's College in New York, the College of Philadelphia, and four of us from Princeton were expected, but I was startled to find among them men from Oxford in England, the Inns of Court in London, Utrecht in Holland, and St. Andrews in Scotland. We were not a bunch of illiterate farmers. We were, said some, 'the pick of the former Colonies.'

> But I was equally impressed by the luminous names I expected to see in our group and didn't.

Patrick Henry was missing and so were the two Adamses from Massachusetts. Tom Jefferson was absent in France. John Marshall wasn't here, nor James Monroe nor John Jay. John Hancock, my father's friend, wasn't here, nor famous Dr. Benjamin Rush. And I expected to see the famous writer and political debater Noah Webster, but he wasn't here.

Eight men were on hand, however, whose presence gave not only Simon Starr but all the other delegates a sense of awe. These were the men who, eleven years before, had dared to sign the Declaration of Independence: these were the men who along with Simon's father had placed their lives in jeopardy to defend the principle of freedom. One by one, these eight introduced themselves to Simon, reminding him of the high esteem in which his father had been held, and he was deeply moved by the experience. Two of the veterans earned a special place in his affections:

I was disappointed on opening day to find that Benjamin Franklin was not present, but on the morning of the second day I heard a commotion in the street outside our meeting hall and some cheering. Running to glimpse what might be happening, I saw coming down the middle of the street an amazing sight, a glassed-in ornate sedan chair of the kind used by European kings.

It hung suspended from two massive poles which rested on the shoulders of eight huge prisoners from the local jail. Inside, perched on pillows, rode an old, baldheaded man who looked like a jolly bullfrog. It was Dr. Franklin, most eminent of the delegates, and the oldest at eighty-one. Gout, obesity and creaking joints made it impossible for him to walk, hence the sedan chair. When the prisoners carried him into the hall, someone alerted him that I was present. Calling 'Halt!' to the prisoners, he beckoned me to approach, and when I did he reached out with both hands to embrace me, and tears came into his eyes: 'Son of a brave man, be like him.'

Franklin, like General Washington, played almost no role in the deliberations; they were ornaments of the most valuable kind, since they reminded the other delegates of the grandeur of the Revolution and the gallant acts that led up to it. There was one more delegate who had signed the Declaration, and he was to become a major influence on Starr:

I was in the assembly hall one morning when I felt a tug on my arm, and turned to see a man I did not know. He was a short, pudgy fellow in his mid-forties, bald and with heavy eye-glasses. There was nothing about his appearance that was memorable, and when he spoke, it was with a heavy Scottish burr which made his words almost unintelligible. 'Hello, lad,' he said. 'Am I right in thinking you're Jared Starr's boy?' When I said I was, he smiled: 'I'm James Wilson, Scotland and Pennsylvania, and I relied upon your father's help at the Declaration of Independence. I suppose your father spoke of me?' Father had said nothing, and I knew nothing about the man who faced me, but as the weeks and months of our assembly passed, this very ordinary-looking man with no oratorical graces emerged as the great solid rock of the Convention, and I noticed that when he spoke, which he did repeatedly, others stopped to listen, for not only was his knowledge encyclopedic but he also talked sense. He was without peer the brains of our effort, for with his merciless logic he killed faulty ideas and with his Scottish enthusiasm he made other men's good ideas palatable. Great orators like Gouverneur Morris of Pennsylvania and Dr. William Samuel Johnson of Connecticut made fiery speeches, half of them wrong, but James Wilson in his quiet way was always right, and after he had been knocked down for six days in a row, he rose on the seventh with fresh arguments to win the day. If our Constitution is a workable success, it is so largely because Wilson hammered its ideas into shape.

Simon was aware that his journal notes now said that

two men were of prime influence on his voting in the
Convention, Hamilton and Wilson, so he added a
note lest someone judge him to have been fickle in
his loyalties:

> I am aware that I said Hamilton was my guide,
> and now I'm saying that Wilson was. The ex-
> planation is simple. The New York delegation
> consisted of three men, Hamilton and two oth-
> ers, but these two scorned what the Convention
> was struggling to do and after a few days they
> stalked out in a huff and never returned. That
> left poor Hamilton high and dry, for as I said,
> we voted by states, and with two of New York's
> three delegates gone, the state could never have
> a quorum. Thus, one of the most brilliant men
> in the nation was left without a vote, so in dis-
> gust he rode back to New York, being absent
> during the sweltering days when men like Mad-
> ison, Mason and Wilson hammered out the cru-
> cial details. So it's simple. Hamilton was not
> present, Wilson was, and I followed the won-
> derfully sane and solid leadership of the latter.

And now we come to a mystery which has given all
subsequent Starrs considerable embarrassment. During the entire hundred and sixteen days of the sessions, and some of the debate was so vigorous that
it became almost violent, Simon Starr uttered not
one word. He attended every session, followed the

swing of debate with close attention, and discussed the nuances at night in the Indian Queen, but in the hall itself he said nothing.

As I sought to know him, over the centuries, I thought: How could an honor graduate from Princeton, a man with his own considerable library, participate at the heart of a world-shattering debate and make no contribution? He himself wondered:

> There were eight of us delegates who said nothing or little. William Blount of North Carolina, Nicholas Gilman of New Hampshire, Richard Bassett of Delaware, William Few of Georgia, John Blair of Virginia, Thomas Mifflin and Robert Morris of Pennsylvania, and me. We kept silent, I think, because we were in the presence of our betters, men who had either wide experience like Dr. Franklin or profound intellectual insights like Madison and Wilson. We felt no urge to parade our ignorance.

> We left the podium open for polished debaters like Gouverneur Morris and Roger Sherman of Connecticut, who spoke upwards of a hundred and forty times each. Careful students of history and politics like Madison and Wilson invariably had something cogent to say on every subject. We eight didn't.

On the matter of speaking, Simon left one paragraph

which has astounded later generations, especially those of us who have gone through public flagellations such as Watergate and the present Iranian arms scandal:

> One of the first decisions agreed upon when we finally assembled was that our deliberations would be conducted in secrecy. News journals would be allowed no entry to our hall and all members promised to disclose nothing of our debate. So for one hundred and sixteen days, fifty-five men who were among the leaders of our nation met and argued and retired to our inns to continue the debate, and we dealt with the most profound topics that men can deal with, the problems of self-government, and not a single clue as to what we were discussing or how we were dividing was revealed to the outside world. Thus, delegates were freed from posturing for public acclaim; more important, they were free to change their minds and to retreat from weak positions hastily taken. I once heard Gouverneur Morris argue heatedly on five different sides of a question in four successive days, coming down finally on the correct side.

So much for the chitchat. It is valuable in that it throws a warm, illuminating light on the delegates and the soul-shattering work they were engaged in, but it is more important that we see how these powerful men grappled with the great problems of their day, and in the Starr family we have always been proud of our ancestor's secret role in the Constitution's greatest victory—ashamed of his part in its most disgraceful defeat.

I said there were fifty-five delegates to the Convention; there were actually two additional 'members,' shadows who cast their silent votes in almost every deliberation. They were Daniel Shays, the Massachusetts revolutionary, and Cudjoe, the black slave imported from the African coast. Whenever the argument between the three big states, who felt entitled to more voice in government, and the several small ones, who demanded protection of their rights, became so heated that compromise became impossible, someone would mention Dan Shays, and the possibility of similar rebellion throughout the states became real. Then tempers subsided, debate continued in a lower key, and men began seriously to reconsider how they could resolve this dilemma of how to allow the big states to exercise the power which they unquestionably had and to which they were entitled without engulfing the small. So Dan Shays, invisible, played a vital role.

One June evening, after a steamingly hot day of bitter debate, Simon Starr was quaffing an ale in the Indian Queen when he saw a group of delegates, some who had spoken on the floor, but most, like himself, silent, and as he started to speak, he drew them about him: 'Let us hoe away all the manure and see what roots grow basically. I'll go first.'

Wetting his lips and pushing back his red hair with both hands, he said: 'It is engraved in granite, fused inseparably to the mountains of our land, that the three big states, Massachusetts, Pennsylvania and Virginia, will never again agree to the old pattern of one state, one vote. That is the bedrock from which we start.'

But a delegate from Delaware, an inoffensive man who also said nothing in public debate, argued: 'As remorseless as the tides of the ocean which no power on earth can halt, the small states will never agree to a legislature in which we do not have equal representation with the big states, and that means one state, one vote.'

'But if you small states persist,' Simon warned, 'we, the more populous states, will simply go home, form a kind of union of our own, and let you small ones join up later when you come to your senses.'

The Delaware man and his supporters did not tremble at the threat: 'If we are denied justice, we'll march out and build an alliance with some European nation.'

Such terrible words, words which shook the soul and made it cringe in despair, could not have been offered in the general assembly, but they deserved airing, and in Simon Starr's informal group, there they stood in naked force, big and little both threatening: Do it my way or we'll go home.

It was beyond the power of young Starr to engineer a compromise between these two adamant positions, but he had sense enough to appreciate the gravity of the impasse faced by the nation. So he sought out delegates from the middle-sized states, and this threw him into the arms of men from Connecticut and South Carolina, who listened attentively as he reported the iron-hard determination of each side not to yield. In the next days the argument reached the floor of the Convention, where tempers were guarded but concessions nonexistent.

Finally, a committee was appointed whose members were dedicated to finding a compromise between large and small, and under the leadership of Roger Sherman, a plan was devised unlike any other that had ever been in existence: the powerful legislature would be divided into two houses, an upper whose members would be appointed by state legislatures, with each state regardless of size having one member, and a lower elected by the general population, with each state entitled to a varying number of members depending on an index of population and wealth, or taxes paid. Some wanted the upper house to be appointed for life, all agreed that the lower house should enjoy certain unique privileges. It was as delicate a balance as could have been devised, and Simon Starr, silent by day, had been a chief instigator by night.

Of course, details had to be perfected slowly and in heated debate. For example, the membership of the lower house was set arbitrarily at fifty-six seats: Virginia would have nine; Pennsylvania, eight; Massachusetts, seven. New Hampshire would have two, and Delaware and Rhode Island, one each. Few delegates liked the distribution, but after protracted discussion a clever correction was proposed which seemed to make everyone happy: the number of seats in the lower house was raised from fifty-six to sixty-five, so distributed as to minimize the strength of the big states and increase the middle group.

The great compromise was in order, the best that could have been devised, and on Monday, 16 July 1787, came the crucial vote, and it was terrifyingly close, as Simon remembered in his memorandum:

As time for voting approached, those of us in favor of a strong, new government grew frightfully nervous, because only a few states were eligible to vote and we knew that the two big states, Virginia and Pennsylvania, were against us, while the third big one, Massachusetts, could not vote at all, since its delegation was evenly split. New York, of course, had no vote during most of the Convention because two of its three delegates had left early in a huff. Think of it! Alexander Hamilton, one of the architects of our nation, had no vote in its building, because New York could never provide a quorum of its delegates! Rhode Island had refused from the first to participate in any way, and poor New Hampshire never collected enough money to send us its two delegates till the summer was waning and our work nearly done.

So, in what might be called the most important vote in the history of our nation, only nine states took part, and in the counting I felt sick when the first three votes were negative. Then it was tied, then it was four against and one more negative would doom us, but the last two votes were yeas. The nation was saved by a vote of five of the little states out of thirteen, and that night I got drunk.

After he sobered up, Simon reflected first on the great moral victory of that day, when delegates submerged their regional prejudices to form a union, and then on the moral cowardice of those same delegates, including himself:

We have refused like cravens to even mention the word that haunts our nation. We delay and avoid and postpone, and if we continue to ignore our reponsibilities, this problem will stay with us and worsen until it destroys this nation.

He was speaking, of course, of slavery, that dark and brooding presence which haunted all discussion and lurked in each meeting corner. Cudjoe the slave emerged everywhere, and the sullen problems he represented were discussed, solved, rejected, and discussed again, the second or third solution being little better than the first in technical terms and usually worse where the moral posture of a great nation was concerned.

Of the original fifty-five delegates, some eighteen owned slaves, and of the signers, a dozen did. Some had only a few; others like George Mason, who abhorred slavery and favored manumission, had many. Washington was a slave owner, as were the two Pinckneys, Charles and Charles Cotesworth, and John Rutledge of South Carolina. Starr, whose family had always owned slaves and who had inherited seventeen prime hands, had inherited also a strong Virginia prejudice in favor of the institution, but his experiences at Princeton as a student and now in Philadelphia as a delegate had begun to make him insecure as to the future. Also, he found it both fascinating and perplexing that Washington had freed some of his slaves and that Mason looked upon slavery as a curse, despite his many slaves.

'I'd be ready to free my slaves,' he told his Southern friends at the Indian Queen, 'if only some way could be worked out to have them keep tending the fields,' but as soon as he said this, his friends started to argue. One said, in sharp comment: 'There are really three Americas; our problem is to keep them all happy. The North, without slaves; the Deep South, which needs them for cotton and sugar; and lucky states like North Carolina, Virginia and Maryland, which have them but whose climates are so kind, they could manage without them.'

A clever man from Georgia pointed out something Simon had not considered before: 'In Georgia and the hot lands west we must continue to import slaves. We'd be strangled if their importation was ended, as you suggested last night. But in Virginia? You'd make money if the importation was halted, because then you could ship the slaves you no longer need down to Georgia and sell them at great profit. As far as we're concerned, you Virginians are as bad as the New Englanders.'

As the debate, formal and informal, continued, Simon learned that the Convention could not escape dealing with four difficult slavery problems: Should it be outlawed altogther? If it was allowed to continue, should further importation from Africa be permitted? If a slave ran away from a plantation in the South to freedom in the North, would the federal government be obligated to return him to his rightful owner? And, most perplexing of all, should the slave be counted as the equal of the white man in allocating taxes and awarding seats in Congress? Debate on these inflammable questions produced some appalling statements.

John Rutledge argued that religion and humanity had nothing to do with the importation of slaves. Financial interest alone was the governing principle with nations. And if the Northern states considered this carefully, they would not oppose the bringing in of more slaves, because the more slaves in the South, the more goods Northern traders would sell.

Pierce Butler of South Carolina wanted the Constitution to state that fugitive slaves who sought freedom in the North were to be delivered like criminals to their owners in the South.

And speaker after speaker hammered home the point that slaves were property, just like other material found on a plantation, and the South required assurance that their owners would be protected in their ownership and use of said property.

Roger Sherman voiced the question that perplexed many Northerners: 'Why should slaves, who are considered property in the South, be counted, when seats are being allocated, any more than cattle and horses in the North?'

General Charles C. Pinckney had an inventive answer: 'To include blacks equally with whites in determining representation is nothing more than justice. For the blacks are the peasants of the Southern states and are as productive of wealth as the laborers of the North. They add equally to the wealth of the nation, and, if you consider money as the sinews of war, to the strength of the nation. It would also be advantageous to the North, since the more representation the Southern states have, the more taxation they will pay.'

Gouverneur Morris came out vigorously against slavery: 'It is a nefarious institution. It is the curse of heaven on the states where it prevails.' He said he would rather pay a tax to free all the Negroes in the United States than to see pro-slavery articles in the Constitution.

Such tirades infuriated William Richardson Davie of North Carolina, who said it was high time to speak out. If the delegates refused to count blacks as at least three-fifths, the business of the Convention was at an end, and he intimated that North Carolina would withdraw.

Of course, it was Gouverneur Morris who leaped up to challenge this threat of dissolution: 'It has been said that it is high time to speak out. I will candidly do so. I came here to form a compact for the good of America. I am ready to do so with all the states. I hope, and believe, that all will enter into such a compact. If they will not, I am ready to join with any states that will.' This was as grave a threat as Davie's, but now Morris, in his ingratiating way, doubled back on all he had said previously, providing an image of urbane sweetness and conciliation. He said that since the compact was to be voluntary, it was vain for the Northern states to insist on demands that the Southern states would never agree to, and it was equally vain for the Southern states to require what the others could never admit, and so on, and so on.

His bland efforts at conciliation proved fruitless, and when Starr met with his cabal at the Indian Queen, he found both the Southerners and the Northerners ready to break apart if their prejudices were not honored. Realizing that the Convention was in peril, he sought out Madison, and found, to his surprise, that this Virginia stalwart was in favor of naming a time limit after which the importation of slaves would be outlawed, suggesting 1800 as an acceptable date. Starr hurried back to his friends: 'I think a compromise is possible,' and a negative one was worked out: Congress could not ban importation prior to 1808 for those states existing in 1787, but it would be under no obligation to do so then.

On the question of capturing runaway slaves who had gained their freedom and returning them to their bondage, the South won. The Constitution required this shameful act to be done.

And then came the crucial question, the one involving morality, political power, tax money and the sanctity of private property. Division of opinion was clear-cut and regional. In allocating seats in the lower house of Congress, the South wanted each slave to be counted as one citizen, but the North argued: 'If the slave has no political rights, he can't be a citizen.' Before this extremely emotional issue was solved, the South argued: 'Since slaves are not citizens, they should not be counted when assessing federal taxes' but the North reasoned: 'We allocate taxes according to the count of the population, and whether a man is a citizen or not is beside the point.'

As Simon explained one night to the other silent members of the Convention: 'The South wants votes but no taxes. The North wants us to pay taxes but have no votes. We may break up on this one.' The debate was prolonged and brilliant, with men of deep conviction wrestling with this most complex of problems. In the end, a subtle compromise was reached, one with the gravest moral flaws but one which allowed the two sections of the nation to remain together for the time being.

When up-to-date census figures were provided for the giving of seats and the collection of taxes, five black slaves would count as three white persons. There was no sensible justification for such a deal, but it was the best that could be worked out in 1787, and it would preserve the nation until 1861, when a civil war would rectify the matter—in blood.

And now a most curious thing happened. Throughout a long summer, these fifty-five delegates had debated the slavery issue, using the word *slave* thousands of times, but when they were required to put their conclusions in writing, all of them, North and South alike, shied away from placing the word *slave* in what they were beginning to consider a sacred document. Men spoke urgently against using the word, but none gave the honest reason: that it would be totally improper to defile a document dedicated to freedom with a word which demonstrated that a large portion of the persons covered were not free.

On the night it was decided, Simon Starr wrote in his notes:

> How shameful the circumlocutions we resorted to. Imported blacks from Africa are not slaves. They are 'such Persons as any of the States now existing shall think proper to admit.' We were afraid to say simply 'Fugitive slaves shall be returned to bondage,' for the words were too ugly. Instead, we devised this beautiful evasion: 'No Person held to Service or Labour in one State, under the Laws thereof, escaping into

another, shall, in Consequence of any Law or Regulation therein, be discharged from such Service or Labour, but shall be delivered up on Claim of the Party to whom such Service or Labour may be due.' What in the world do such words mean? What crimes do they mask?

Simon was not proud of himself or his colleagues that night.

These informal evening discussions were never attended by three of the outstanding delegates: General Washington was too busy with the social leaders of Philadelphia; Benjamin Franklin was too infirm; and James Madison, the aloof scholar, remained in his room, mysteriously occupied. But one night Madison suddenly appeared at the edge of the group, a small unimpressive fellow in his late thirties, with a penetrating eye and a manner which indicated that he did not suffer fools easily.

'Starr,' he said in a voice so low that few could hear, and when Simon joined him he said nothing but indicated that they should move to his room. When the door was closed behind them, Starr saw a jumble of papers on and beside a low writing desk. Unable to imagine why Madison had summoned him, he turned to ask, when Madison said with the warmest interest: 'I wasn't aware you had attended the college in Princeton,' and the friendly manner in which the words were spoken encouraged Simon to ask: 'You, too?'

Yes, some eight years before Simon attended that fine Presbyterian school to which so many Southern boys migrated, Madison had gained distinction there by his exceptional work; but now, as he and Simon talked about their college years, Madison said modestly: 'Studies were easy. I went back for an extra year to take Hebrew and ethics.'

'Why?'

'A man must know many things . . . many different things.' He reflected on this, then added: 'When I was a member of the Continental Congress, and now here, I do believe I used each single item of history and philosophy and ethics I learned at college.'

'And Hebrew?'

'Studies like Hebrew toughen the mind.'

'I've noticed in debate that you have a very organized mind.'

'Why don't you speak up? I'm told you're effective in the night debates?'

Starr bowed and asked an impertinent question: 'When were you born, Mr. Madison?'

'In 1751.'

'You're only eight years older than me. It seems impossible.'

'Ah, Mr. Starr. Don't despair. Those years were spent in constant study. And now I seek your help as a very bright young gentleman. On something I wrote some nights ago.' With that, he lifted from his table a hefty stack of sheets containing meticulously written paragraphs and dated Monday, June 18. The entry began: 'MR. HAMILTON had hitherto been silent on the business before the Convention, partly from respect to others 'whose superior abilities, age and experience rendered him unwilling to bring forward ideas dissimilar to theirs . . .'

'You're a friend of the colonel's, are you not?' Madison asked, and Simon replied without hesitating: 'I revere him.'

'Good! And you heard the long speech he delivered before he returned to New York?'

'I did.'

'You have my notes summarizing what I thought he said. I want you to read them carefully and point out any spots at which my memory might be doing him an injustice.'

'Why?'

'Because I was appalled at the strong monarchical nature of his recommendations—his obsequious respect for all things British.'

'Sometimes there is that cast to his thought,' Simon confessed, remembering his discussions with Hamilton. 'But I didn't think his remarks in the Convention . . .'

'Good! As a friend of his, please show me where I might have introduced error.'

Simon often told acquaintances of that extraordinary night of editorial work, but what they remembered most were his concluding remarks:

> So, long into the night, as I read Mr. Madison's careful report of what Colonel Hamilton had said, I sat on one side of the lamp, he on the

other, me reading intently, him writing furiously, and when I finished I asked: 'What are you writing, Mr. Madison?' and he said: 'Each afternoon when the debate ends, I come here and try to report it faithfully speech by speech,' and when I asked why he did this, since we had Major William Jackson as our paid secretary, he said: 'In years to come the Republic may need an honest account of what really transpired.'

So each day Mr. Madison rises early, has a frugal breakfast, reports to the Convention, engages vigorously in debate, speaks far more than most and with better effect, then comes home, dines sparingly, and drafts his account of what happened. He is not required to do this, and when I handed him back the Hamilton pages with the monarchical passages marked either *yes* or *no*, I asked him how many pages his journal covered, and he said with that great precision of mind which marked all he did: 'I calculate there will be about a quarter of a million words.' And all of this completed at night while the rest of us are arguing and drinking beer.

In the latest stages of the long session, Simon added another portrait, which would be widely circulated after the death of both him and his subject:

There was another delegate from Pennsylvania whom I came to know late and unfavorably. I seemed unable to apprehend him, for although he was only seven or eight years older than me, he had acquired such a suave manner, which he displayed at every opportunity, that I both loathed and envied him. He was Gouverneur Morris, big and plump and almost oily, with the habit of reaching out to touch anyone whom he was striving to best in an argument. He spoke far more than anyone else in the Convention, but when I listened closely to what he said, he seemed to come down on all sides of every argument, but he had the effective tactic of admitting at the beginning of one of his amusing speeches that yes, he did yesterday say that he was against this motion but that overnight conversation with those who knew more about it than he had convinced him that he was wrong, and then he would launch into a vigorous defense of his new position. I stopped listening to his first four speeches on any topic, waiting until he reached his fifth position, which sometimes made great sense, for he was not stupid, just lacking in character.

What astounded me about Morris as I followed his wavering career was his effect upon women, for whenever a wife or daughter visited Philadelphia to stay with one of the delegates, there he was, like a gallant from the palace of

Louis XIV paying court and kissing fingertips and uttering compliments that would make an ordinary man blush. He was reputed to be a dashing man with the ladies, and I noticed that when a tavern maid brought him a mug of ale, he treated her with the same exalted courtesy and courtship that he paid the wife of a wealthy businessman, and the tavern maid accepted his graciousness as if it were her right.

All this, mind you, with a withered right arm damaged by boiling water when he was a child and a big, clanking wooden left leg, the consequence of a riding accident in his youth. He was Caliban, and I did not like him.

But Simon penned a second report on Morris, and it has been this one which immortalizes the pompous ladies' man:

By late Saturday afternoon, 8 September 1787, we delegates felt that we had made all the decisions necessary to launch our young nation on a bold new course, but the various papers reporting our conclusions were a sad jumble. So General Washington instructed us to vote in secret for five of our members who would bring order into this chaos. When the votes were counted, five of our ablest men had been chosen, Hamilton and Madison among them, and they were handed the impossible task of setting our new government in order. They were to work Saturday night, all day Sunday, and submit their finished job on Monday—and it did indeed prove to be an impossible task. For on Monday they reported sleepily that they would require one extra day, and it was granted.

To my surprise, Gouverneur Morris had been elected to this august body which would make all the final decisions, but when I asked my friends why, they reminded me: 'He does have a way with words.'

No written account exists of how the committee spent their three nights and two days, but word circulated that the members were aghast when they looked at the jumble of papers before them and realized that they faced twenty-three rambling, disorganized and sometimes contradictory articles which they must fashion into a coherent document. I believe, and so do others, that Morris stepped forward, gathered the mass into his arms, one good, one withered, and sat down to rewrite the whole. The other four, awed by the complexity of the task, were glad to have him try his hand.

Hamilton told me: 'It was Morris who wrote that sterling preamble. He borrowed the phrase *We the People* from an earlier version, but on his own he added the important words *of the United States*. And he alone was responsible for that musket fire of eight short, simple verbs denoting action and determination: form, establish, insure, provide, promote, secure, ordain, establish. Right at the start he wanted the world to know that we meant business.'

Some whispered in the days that followed that Morris had perverted his assignment to his own purposes, slipping back into the final version points he had lost in debate, but none of the other four ever charged him with that. What he did do, all agreed, was tighten any loose statement always to make the powers of the federal government stronger and clearer.

When we ordinary delegates finally received a printed version of what the committee had accomplished and saw with admiration that the twenty-three rambling articles had been compressed into seven of remarkable sharpness, we assumed that this was the work of Hamilton and Madison, but when I quietly congratulated the latter, he corrected me: 'No, it was Gouverneur. He grappled with chaos and brought it into logical order and felicitous style.'

Now that our new government seems a success it has become popular, with those who do not know, to hail Madison as 'The Father of our Constitution.' Those like me who followed closely what actually happened are apt to think it was James Wilson. But regardless of who the father was, the midwife who supervised the birth was Gouverneur Morris, the one-legged dandy. Perhaps every nation, now and then, has need of someone who knows how to use words with precision and emotion.

On Monday, 17 September 1787, forty-one tired but happy delegates met for the last time in the hall that housed their debate. Armed guards still kept away inquisitive strangers, for the pledge of secrecy taken so long ago had been preserved right up to these final moments, and there was an air of excitement as men told one another: 'I think we'll finish today.'

When the session began General Washington astonished everyone by making his first and only speech of the Convention. On all previous days he had sat in silent grandeur as the storms of argument swirled about him, but now he rose to support a motion that membership in the lower house be made more widely democratic, one representative to every thirty thousand population instead of every forty thousand. Wrote Madison later: 'No opposition was made to the proposition, and it was agreed to unanimously.' Washington had a way of enforcing unanimity.

But now came a most painful moment, for as the delegates prepared to cast the momentous vote which would determine the future of their nation, it became apparent that three of the finest, ablest and most intelligent members of the Convention would refuse to sign. In an impassioned cry from the heart, Alexander Hamilton pleaded with the three not to abstain: 'No man's ideas are more remote from the plan than mine are known to be. But is it possible to deliberate between anarchy and convulsion on the one side and the chance of good to be expected from the plan on the other?' He begged the delegates to join with him and sign unanimously.

His plea was futile. Edmund Randolph of Virginia, Elbridge Gerry of Massachusetts and, to the amazement of all, George Mason of Virginia refused to sign, and not even an ardent plea from Dr. Franklin, read by James Wilson, caused them to change their minds.

Forty-one men were in the chamber that morning, three refused to sign, but thirty-nine did. How was that possible? John Dickinson of Delaware had had to leave Philadelphia early, but was so desirous of launching a new government that his fellow delegate from Delaware, George Read, was allowed to execute his proxy.

That night James Madison, still scratching away on his personal journal, penned one of the loveliest paragraphs in American history:

> Whilst the last members were signing, Doctor Franklin, looking toward the President's chair, at the back of which a rising sun happened to be painted, observed to a few members near

him that painters had found it difficult to distinguish in their art, a rising, from a setting, sun. I have, said he, often and often, in the course of the session, and the vicissitudes of hopes and fears as to its issue, looked at that behind the President, without being able to tell whether it was rising or setting; but now at length I have the happiness to know, that it is a rising, and not a setting, sun.

Those were the last words that Madison would write in his journal, and as he worked, the rest of the delegates traipsed over to the City Tavern for a night of feasting, drinking and goodfellowship.

The nation did not rush to embrace the Constitution designed by my ancestor Simon Starr and his thirty-eighty associates. It had been agreed that for it to go into effect, nine states would have to ratify it, but since cantankerous Rhode Island still refused to have anything to do with it, that meant nine out of twelve. If four rejected it, the vast labor would go for naught.

The chronology was frighteningly slow. The finished document was presented to the nation in September 1787. The ninth state to ratify, New Hampshire, did not do so until June 1788. The new government was finally put into place with the inauguration of General Washington as President on 30 April 1789.

Simon Starr made a significant contribution to ratification during the extremely close contest in Massachusetts, where a veteran of Shays' Rebellion harangued the voters with grave condemnations of the proposed Constitution:

> 'It was written by rich men for the protection of their wealth. They keep their slaves. The western lands on which so many of them gambled jump in value, making them all richer still. Their manufactures are protected, and every article in the document favors them and oppresses us. The poor farmer gets no relief, so the Constitution by rich men for the rich should be rejected.'

Friends of the Constitution, grasping for every vote, invited Simon to participate in its defense as the son of the patriot Jared Starr who had died in Massachusetts defending strong government. Like his father before him, he jumped at the chance to help in the North, and at a gathering in Boston he boldly rebutted the opponents:

> 'I own slaves, and I confess that the proposed Constitution protects me in that ownership. I own a few shares in a gamble on western lands, and if you ratify, those lands will grow in value. And I have other small interests which will prosper if we have a strong central government.

But so will all of your interests and the interests of the nation at large. This is what we strove to accomplish in Philadelphia, the improvement of all for the benefit of all, and I think we achieved it.

'Of course, I'm aware that everything we did strengthened my personal holdings, but at the time of voting, that personal interest was never foremost in my mind. Nor was it in the minds of others. We were thirty-nine ordinary men, no more honest nor dishonest than any like thirty-nine that you could find. We labored only to build a strong, new nation able to guide and protect itself, and I think we did just that. Please accept our work. Ratify it and we shall all prosper.'

In a close vote, 187 to 168, Massachusetts became the sixth state to ratify. The logjam was broken, and when three more states followed—Maryland, South Carolina, New Hampshire—the new nation was put upon the right track. In its creation and guidance my forefathers Jared and Simon Starr had played honorable if not conspicuous roles.

It was the final entry in Simon's notes, written in 1807, that seemed to me to strike an honest balance regarding the character of the men who wrote and signed that Constitution:

I find constant pride in what my associates in that great Convention have achieved since we left Philadelphia. Alexander Hamilton was the leading light of the first presidencies, and James Madison served with almost equal brilliance in various posts. I think more than a dozen became United States senators, including four of that group dubbed by the other delegates 'The Silent Ones' who did not venture to speak in debate: Richard Bassett, William Blount, William Few and Nicholas Gilman. John Rutledge became Chief Justice of the Supreme Court and three others served as associates: John Blair, William Paterson and the brilliant James Wilson.

But there were others who did not prosper, and some of their cases are appalling. No one stood higher before the Convention or lower after its close than Robert Morris, the patriotic banker of the American Revolution. When I first met him in 1787, he was whispered to be the richest man in America, with immense holdings in cash and land speculations. But in later years his precarious ventures began to crumble, until he had to sell off most of his holdings. In 1798 his creditors, still unsatisfied, forced him to dispose even of the grand mansion in which he had entertained General Washington during the Convention, but this gained him neither time nor relief. Shocking as it seems even now, this one-time millionaire was tossed into a debtors' prison where he languished for three long years, aided by none of the friends who had earned fortunes by following his advice. Finally, word circulated among the former delegates, and some of us collected enough money to get him out of jail, but he spent his final days in poverty till the age of seventy-three, when he died alone and forgotten.

Four other delegates watched in glum despair as their fortunes declined into bankruptcy, the most pitiful case being that of James Wilson, my hero and an associate justice of the Supreme Court. He had lost so much money gambling on western lands that a swarm of creditors harassed him. To escape a forced bankruptcy, he fled to New Jersey, from where he continued to conduct Court business, to the disgust of all. Finally, his powerful mind having failed, he skipped to North Carolina, where a fellow justice on the Court took pity on him, providing him with a small cottage in which he died, his mind gone, at age fifty-six. I went into mourning when I heard of this great man's fall.

But worse was to come. I was shocked to distraction when I learned that two of my fellow delegates, patriots of the greatest ardor in the summer I knew them, conducted themselves so carelessly that they were actually indicted for treason! Jonathan Dayton of New Jersey became so involved with that archenemy of mankind, Aaron Burr, that he was formally charged with treason, only narrowly escaping trial.

William Blount of North Carolina was serving in the Senate when his enormous land speculations turned so sour that he became entangled in complex and illegal negotiations with Spain, Great Britain and various Indian tribes. When incriminating letters were intercepted he was expelled from the Senate by a vote of 25 to 1. The House then impeached him, but the Senate judged that expulsion was enough, and there it ended.

For me, the Convention ended on a bright July day in 1804 when a messenger came galloping down my lane, shouting: 'Simon! Simon! Have you heard? Alexander Hamilton is dead!' I stood perfectly still, the hot sun beating down upon my face, my senses numbed. Hamilton dead? A young man with the world before him? The architect of our stability as a nation? A victor in actual battle, a constant winner in debate, he was abler than us all, a man I loved for his gallantry and courage. And then came the crushing blow, the one from which I will never recover.

'Simon! It's true. Aaron Burr shot him in a duel. A matter of political honor.' And when the news finally filtered in, I found all that my informant said was true. Alexander Hamilton, the finest man of his generation, was dead by a bullet from the pistol of Aaron Burr, that unspeakable craven, that traitor, that disrupter of nations. My God, that such things are allowed!

Our family has a careful record of what happened after that fateful day in 1804, because Simon's son, Edmund, who would serve on the United States Supreme Court, left a tragic memorandum:

My father Simon spent the rest of 1804 in a trance, unable to focus on anything for long. The death of Hamilton, the man he admired above all others, represented a tragedy he could not absorb. In 1805 he pulled himself together and traveled to Philadelphia, where with the help of Gouverneur Morris, a man whom he had not liked at first but who grew upon him as he did upon all who knew him, arranged a kind of rescue fund for their fellow delegate Robert Morris, whom they found in poverty.

When he returned home at the end of 1805, he fell afoul of a blatant Jeffersonian named

Killbride living in Culpeper, and although they never referred to each other by name, Killbride defamed the memory of Hamilton constantly, accusing him of being a royalist who wanted to install a king in Washington, while my father attacked President Jefferson for being a radical in the pay of France. At a debate in Washington, Killbride finally so infuriated my father by demeaning Hamilton that there was no recourse but to challenge Killbride to a duel, which was eagerly accepted.

Father chose me as his second, and on a gray December morning in 1807 along the banks of the Potomac, eight of us marched into the mists, arranged ourselves as tradition dictated, and prepared for the duel. As seconds, Killbride's man and I had to ask one last time if the difference between the two protagonists could be reconciled, and each man said in firm voice 'No!'

To the tremulous counting of the judge, one to ten, the two men walked away from each other, and I remember thinking: My God, if they could just keep marching forever! But at the count of ten, which rang like a funeral bell, they turned and fired, and my father fell dead with a bullet just above the heart.

So ended his preoccupation with the American Constitution and his adoration of Alexander Hamilton.

That evening as I walked under the trees that he planted on our place, I thought: Thirty-nine signers of our Constitution, two ended as traitors, two murdered in duels. That's ten percent, and I began to chuckle as my red-headed father might have, to recall the charges that he had had to combat in the Massachusetts fight for ratification: that the framers were all rich, all slaveholders, all protectors of privilege.

No! No! They were a collection of ordinary men, some bad, some good, some dull, some bright, some pro-slavery, some anti-slavery, and two of them, Hamilton and my father, ready to surrender their lives in defense of things they believed in.

Justice
Edmund
Starr

1780–1847

IN A PERVERSE WAY, I've always reserved a special affection for one of the least admirable of my ancestors. In physical bulk, Justice Edmund Starr was unquestionably the greatest by at least a hundred and thirty pounds, but intellectually, I'm afraid he was a midget. Like others of our family, he first achieved public attention because of his valor in battle defending our nation, but it is not for such early feats that he's in the history books. I cherish him because he illustrates how men or women of only modest attainment can sometimes take part in major accomplishments; in his case, help to keep society on the right path in times of decision. Justice Starr hoisted his immense bulk onto the bench of the United States Supreme Court at a time when a loyal, reliable vote like his was needed, and in his own way he helped forge the concepts that bound our nation together, and so when I returned from the White House tired and frightened on Friday night, I certainly did not want to distress Nancy with speculation about what might happen at my Monday appearance before the Senate Committee. Instead, I found quiet solace in ruminating with her about the amusing judicial experiences of our less than illustrious ancestor.

A rural neighbor once said of Edmund Starr: 'To settle a wager as to whether he weighed more than three hundred and twenty-five, we put him on the scale I use for hogs, and he tipped at three twenty-three.' A fellow justice inclined toward the radical views of Thomas Jefferson characterized him as 'flabby in both body and mind,' while the keeper of an inn in Washington said: 'His great love is dark brown ale, which he consumes in prodigious draughts.'

Chief Justice John Marshall, the one whose opinion counted, wrote of him:

No matter how contentious the debate became, nor how the general population or the Jeffersonians railed against the Court, I could always depend upon the support of Justice Starr. Frequently he could not fully comprehend the intricacies of a case, and sometimes he even got the sides of a question entangled, so that he did not know whether he was supporting the claimant or the government, but when I explained the niceties he accepted my analysis and voted in accord with the principles I was endeavoring to establish.

Starr had not always been obese, or even obtuse. As a slim young Virginia farmer in 1799, he had decided one day 'I want to be a lawyer,' so without formal training of any kind, not even working in the office of an established lawyer, he attended court, read a few books, and offered himself as a counselor. His good humor and common sense enabled him to prevail in country courthouses, and when he traipsed off to war in 1812 against the British, he left behind a lucrative practice. He joined the Virginia militia in time to take part in three straight American losses, but demonstrated such willingness and courage that he gained promotion to captain and then to major.

Fighting always in the eastern theater of this disastrous war, he attracted the attention of James Monroe, the Secretary of War, and when Monroe attained the presidency he appointed Starr to the Supreme Court.

I think in some ways he summarizes the Starrs. Always ready to serve the Army. Seldom out front or showing off in public. And for some strange reason, happiest when we follow the lead of someone more notable than ourselves. Jared, in the arguments that led to the Declaration, said little but followed the lead of Ben Franklin. His son Simon, at the great Convention, said never a word but did listen to Hamilton. And *his* son, the justice, sat through a dozen historic cases without asking a question, but when the Chief Justice needed support, there he was. As for me, I follow Ronald Reagan. He won forty-nine of the fifty states, didn't he?

So this huge fellow sat on the Supreme Court, listening and dozing while Marshall and Story picked arguments apart and asked lawyers probing questions. 'He is like a great sleeping walrus,' said one newspaper, 'waiting for a fish to swim by,' and so he appeared in several cartoons of the time, his drooping mustaches converting him into a gross human being topped by a walrus head. In a letter to his wife he explained the affinity which had grown up between him and Marshall:

> He finds himself comfortable with me because neither of us ever studied law. We just became lawyers on our own. Then, too, he was never a judge, leapfrogged right into the job of Chief Justice. He told the Court the other day: 'I

think and think and make the right decision, then leave it to Justice Story here to cite the precedents on which it should have been made. He's a scholar, I'm not.'

In the February term of 1819, Justice Starr was privileged to sit through what legal scholars call 'the six most important weeks in the history of any major court,' for in a series of thunderbolt decisions, Chief Justice Marshall and his six associates hammered into place the rules under which the nation would henceforth be governed: 'At the close of this breathless period, Marshall told me: "Starr, a constitution is a bundle of flabby wishes till the courts give it a backbone." ' The United States would never be the same after these blazing weeks.

There was a more fundamental reason why Starr and Marshall functioned so amiably. They both despised Tom Jefferson. Marshall often carried in his pocket that incredible statement about Shays' Rebellion which Jefferson had issued from the safety of his cushy job in Paris:

God forbid we should ever be twenty years without such a rebellion. What country can preserve its liberties if their rulers are not warned from time to time that their people preserve the spirit of resistance. Let them take arms! What signify a few lives lost in a century or two? The tree of liberty must be refreshed from

time to time with the blood of patriots and ty-
rants. It is its natural manure.

'Imagine a man like that as President!' Marshall
grumbled. 'Our task is to frustrate the radicalism he
introduced,' and the two justices strained every mus-
cle to do just that.

They started with the famous *Dartmouth College*
v. *Woodward* case, in which Marshall established the
sanctity of contracts, a decision enabling the business
of the nation to proceed and grow in an orderly way
for the next hundred years. What role did our justice
play in this crucial case? He seems not to have followed the impassioned argument, focusing instead
on the appearance of the principal lawyer, Daniel
Webster. Making no comment whatever on the mer-
its of the case, Starr wrote to a friend:

> Daniel Webster came before us like a leading
> actor in a play. Robust, handsome, shoes of the
> most expensive quality, tight britches of a pur-
> plish color, blue cloth coat fitted exquisitely to
> his frame and adorned with flashing silver or
> pewter buttons, a waistcoat uniting with a huge
> expanse of ruffled shirt, a flowing collar marked
> by an elaborate kerchief, hair neatly tied in a
> tail behind. When he spoke, he dominated the
> Court.

It was Justice Starr who was responsible for the lasting picture we have of Webster as he concluded his plea in defense of Dartmouth's right to exist under its contract:

> When Webster finished, he stood silent before our Court. Then in his great organ voice told us: 'You may destroy this little institution: it is weak, it is in your hands. You may put it out. But if you do so, you must extinguish, one after another, all those great lights of science which have thrown their radiance over this land. It is, sir, as I have said, a small college. And yet there are those who love it.' When he finished, there were tears in his eyes, and in mine, too. We all voted in his favor, and I think Dartmouth College was saved, but it might have been the other way.

Justice Starr played a similar role in what is widely regarded as the most important case ever to be decided by the Court, *McCulloch* v. *Maryland*, but like many commentators at the time and since, he seemed to have difficulty in remembering who was claiming what and the significance of the arguments. It came down to two questions on which the future of our nation depended: First, is the federal government denied permission to create a needed agency, in this case a national bank, if the Constitution overlooked granting such a power, or can Congress rely upon authorizations not spelled out but implied by common sense? Second, and of even greater import, can a state, in this case Maryland, impose excessive taxes on an agency created by the federal government and thus destroy it? Put simply, what body of law controls the United States—the rigid terms of a Constitution engraved in stone in 1787, or a living, breathing body of principles, always loyal to the framework of the Constitution but able to adjust to the nation's evolving needs?

Webster and a scintillating Maryland lawyer named William Pinkney defended the government, but once again Justice Starr missed the essential arguments, even Webster's immortal cry: 'The power to tax is the power to destroy.' He also missed most of Pinkney's historic three-day oration, which Justice Joseph Story, sitting in the case, called 'the greatest effort I have ever heard.' What Starr concentrated on once more was sartorial splendor:

> I perceived that he [Pinkney] wore a corset to squeeze in a belly which was even bigger than mine. He also wore women's powder and grease to handsome up his face, shoes high-heeled to make him taller, and suitings, changed each day, to bedazzle the ladies in the gallery and the judges on the bench. He dazzled me.

Starr could not report on Pinkney's inspired arguments in favor of a strong, central government, because, as the papers revealed: 'Pinkney's arguments on the first day must have satisfied Justice Starr, who slept through much of the second day and some of the third.' But after the decision was read, only three days after argument, Chief Justice Marshall told a friend: 'I could not have written this difficult decision judgment without the assistance of Starr, who sat with me for three long days and nights, caring for my pages as I finished them and bringing me refreshment.'

And what were Marshall's answers to the two burning questions? That the government could operate on implied powers, thus adjusting to new needs and conditions as they arose. Therefore, even though the Constitution said not one word about the right of the central government to establish a national bank supervising the currency, common sense, as Alexander Hamilton had reasoned, dictated that the federal government must have that power. And that in the vital areas defined by the Constitution, the powers of the federal government prevailed over those of the states. Of course, it would be profitable to Maryland if she could tax operations of the federal government carried on within her boundaries, but the rights of the central had to supersede; also, each state would be tempted to impose duties upon the goods of other states coming into it, but the federal government could not allow the confusion that would result. When these matters were finally clarified for Edmund Starr, he exulted in letters home: 'I think

I have helped John Marshall save the nation. We can now march forward.'

But the picture of Justice Starr which I treasure is one written by an Englishman traveling through his former colonies:

> The judges of the Supreme Court meet in Washington part of the year, then serve as circuit judges during the remainder. Chief Justice Marshall is responsible for Virginia and North Carolina; Justice Starr for South Carolina and Georgia. It is their delight, at the end of their circuits, to meet in Richmond, where they engage in a protracted challenge of quoits covering three or four days. The Chief Justice is now near eighty, but as bright of eye as a man of thirty. Justice Starr is a quarter of a century younger, and of such enormous girth that he requires a colored boy to reach down and fetch him his quoits, round iron saucers with big holes in the middle.

> You should hear these eminent jurists compete. Standing side by side at one end of the pit, they pair themselves with local gentlemen at the other end, which means that the two justices compete one against the other. Their shouts can be heard at a distance, and there are noisy arguments as to whose quoit is nearer the meg.

I did notice, however, that when the Chief Justice made a particularly good throw, the players agreed that his was best, even though Starr's was clearly closer, and although Marshall must have been aware of this favoritism, he accepted it as his due.

When the game ended, with him invariably the winner, players and spectators alike repaired to a tent to gorge ourselves on barbecue, a delicious concoction of roasted pork and peppery sauce, assisted by melons and fruits, all washed down with glasses of toddy, punch and porter, followed by a rich dessert called mince pie.

It is difficult for the English visitor to realize that these two unpretentious old men in shirt sleeves determine the legal fate of our thirteen former colonies and the eleven new states which have recently joined them.

General
Hugh
Starr

1833–1921

ON SATURDAY, Nancy insisted that we avoid a big lunch and go instead to the Georgetown Racquet Club for some vigorous tennis with the Wrightsons, and I appreciated the suggestion, because although I'm always too lazy to make such a decision myself, when Nancy arranges it, I accept. It helps keep the weight down, and on this tense day, the anxiety.

Sam Wrightson was considerate, for although he

is on the staff of the *Washington Post*, he did not pester me with questions about the rumors of my role in the Iran or Nicaragua affair. It was a lively game, interrupted most pleasantly at the end of the first set by the unexpected appearance of Zack McMaster, who apologized to the Wrightsons: 'I hoped I'd find these characters here. Could I please speak to them for a moment?'

'When legal eagles scream, we salute,' Wrightson said, and off they went to fetch some lemonade.

'Nothing important,' Zack told us. 'I'm afraid I've been a little uptight these last few days. May have made you nervous. No need. No need at all.' He accented these last two words quite heavily, then added: 'I'm meeting this afternoon with some of the older men in our firm . . . to nail things down. So you relax.'

It was the kind of assurance I needed, and I remember our last set that day as some of the most enjoyable tennis we've had. Back home, after we'd showered, I told Nancy: 'We ought to do that more often,' and she exploded with laughter: 'Look who's talking more tennis, you lazy bum.' For lunch we had whole-wheat toast, a tangy cheddar cheese and big glasses of cold buttermilk, after which Nancy said she wanted to query me about one of my ancestors whom she did not care much for, because of his cavalier treatment of women, but whom I respected as one of the best.

Whether she really wanted to know about the general or was merely trying to keep me distracted, I'm not sure, but we did talk.

On no member of the Starr family did the Constitution fall with a heavier hand than on Hugh Starr, for he found himself far ahead of its provisions and had to wait painfully until amendments were made.

It was in the summer of 1856, while serving as instructor at West Point, trim in appearance and sharp of mind, that he became personally aware that the Union was in real danger of flying apart. Two bodies of information reached him from two much different sources. First came a detailed letter from his older brother, who had remained at home in Virginia to operate the small holding known affectionately as the 'family plantation.' The brothers had inherited from their father, the Supreme Court justice, some eight hundred acres and thirteen slaves, and to tend the place effectively, they had acquired an additional six slaves, and it was these nineteen that were causing concern:

> Hugh, I'm perplexed by the damages the South suffers from its adherence to slavery. It brings us constant criticism from church groups and abolitionists, even though we can morally justify our behavior, because you and I know that we treat our slaves decently. But dispensing with the system would take a moral burden off our backs. More significant is the fact that some

of the wisest men of northern Virginia and those who operate the best plantations and large farms have come to a striking conclusion. Counting the cost of everything we have to provide a slave, clothing, medicine, food and a place to live, we would get a much better deal for ourselves by setting them free and hiring them back for a small cash wage. Think about this. I recommend it, and so do the others.

When Hugh tried to reconcile such a radical shift with his emotional support of his home state, he was always left with one stubborn idea: Slavery is the way we define the South. Virginia can't turn its back on slavery and remain Virginia, but my brother's right. Change is inescapable. Unable to resolve the dilemma, he could make no sensible reply to his brother's suggestion that the Starrs rid themselves of their burden: It may make sense economically but not in daily living. He would postpone his decision.

But he was also required to adjust his thinking about the North, because four of his fellow officers, 'almost the best of the lot' he decided, came from Vermont, Massachusetts, New York and Pennsylvania, and in nightly discussions they presented such a rational, nonhysterical body of opinion that he had to listen. They were not abolitionists and voiced little patience with those who were, nor did they display any animus against the South, but Starr was surprised at how firm they were in their opposition to slavery.

The man from Vermont, Captain Benjamin Greer, was a wiry, taciturn fellow, a year or so older than Starr and not given to ranting. So when Greer said one night: 'If the differences between slave states and free continue to widen, the Union could possibly divide, break clean apart,' Starr was appalled that an officer in the United States Army dared make such a seditious statement. But when the four Northerners pressed him as to what choice he might make in such a situation, he had to confess: 'In my family it's always been Virginia first, the Union second. So I suppose I'd have to follow whatever lead Virginia took.'

Greer, seeing Hugh's perplexity, assured him: 'I'm not threatening to shatter the Union, never, never. But as I listen to you Southern men talk, I hear you advocating positions that can only lead to a split between the two sections of our nation.'

'Sad day that would be,' Hugh said, dismissing the possibility, but when he listened closely to what officers from Carolina and Alabama were whispering, he was forced into a gloomy conclusion: Yes, I can imagine a mess when Virginians like me might be goaded into forming a union of our own where the traditions of the South would be preserved. And once he conceded this about himself, he saw that responsible Northerners like Ben Greer were edging toward a similar solution: In order to defend what they believe in, they may also decide that they'll have to have a union of their own. He was frightened by this collision—or separation—course.

His vague reflections were dispelled by the arrival of a bugle-call letter which demanded that he make up his mind, for his brother wrote:

> Hugh, I've made the decision for us, and unless you countermand it by an immediate letter, I shall proceed. All of us who occupy the good lands at the bend of the river have decided to manumit our slaves, hire them back for wages, and give each family a plot of our land big enough to sustain themselves. This will not only release us from increasingly difficult moral problems, but will also make our return on our land considerably more profitable . . .

The startling letter contained many additional details, most of which Hugh judged to be in the interests of everyone, white owner and black slave alike. Because Ben Greer was interested in such matters, Hugh sought him out, placed the letter before him, and said: 'I want you to see how we Southerners react to the problems you've been discussing.' The social statesmanship of the Virginia letter was so pronounced and the personal integrity of the farmers involved so clear that Greer summoned his Northern friends and read them the details.

'It's magnificent that your brother can think so clearly,' Greer said. 'I suppose you'll be sending him your approval?'

'Yes,' and that night he showed Greer the letter he had composed:

> You have my permission. I turn over to you all my rights in the nineteen Starr slaves with the understanding that you will manumit the lot. But regardless of how the details are arranged, I hope you can see to it that my personal slave Hannibal remains with me, if the cost is not prohibitive.

Hugh's letter was quite long, because he went into detail about each of the family units among the Starr slaves: 'Birdsong and Nelly are too old to work regularly for a salary, and since they can't live much longer . . . How old is Birdsong, in his nineties maybe? Arrange for him and Nelly to take their meals with one of the other families and charge it to me.'

Quiet word, all of it approving, passed through West Point regarding the extraordinary act of young Starr in freeing his slaves. Even die-hard officers from South Carolina and Georgia stopped by his quarters to voice their reserved sanction. Said one confirmed Southerner with a degree from Oxford: 'Louisiana and Mississippi aren't ready yet to do what you've done. For the present we need our slaves. It's been proved that in those swampy, steamy climates no white man can possibly work outdoors in the sun. So without our slaves we'd have no sugar or rice. But even so, I do believe that if the Northerners leave us alone, we'll probably free all our slaves by the early years of the next century, when we'll continue to produce sugar and rice with freed Negro help.'

As the young officers at West Point gingerly edged toward a mutual understanding regarding slavery, they were unaware that in Washington the Supreme Court was also belatedly attempting to correct the tragic errors left in the Constitution by the framers seventy years earlier. Now the justices would specify how the United States must handle slavery. These were the tense weeks of February 1857, when Franklin Pierce was ending his presidency and James Buchanan was about to begin his, and although the Court had decided what its judgment was going to be, the justices realized that it would be inflammatory, so they delayed announcing it until Buchanan had been safely inaugurated.

This took place on a frosty fourth of March, and two days later the Supreme Court delivered one of its most poisonous decisions, *Dred Scott* v. *Sanford*. Facts in the case were simple and uncontested: Dred Scott, a Missouri slave, sixty-two years old, had been taken by his owner north into free territory. After a prolonged stay there as a free man, Dred voluntarily returned to Missouri, where he was promptly claimed as a slave by his former owner's widow. The problems: Was Dred in any sense of the word a citizen? Had he the right to sue in a federal court? And did return to slave territory automatically reinstall him as a slave?

The major opinion was read by the Chief Justice,

immediate successor to the awesome John Marshall and a jurist almost as revered. He was Roger Brooke Taney, a tall, thin, acidulous legal scholar from Maryland, eighty years old and passionately dedicated to the task of protecting the gallant agrarian South against the grubby industrial North. In his crusade he was abetted by five other members of his nine-man court who also sided with the Southern states; the seventh justice vacillated in his loyalties, while numbers eight and nine were outspokenly Northern in their sympathies.

It required all the first day for Taney to read his extensive review of slavery in the United States, and when he finished, his audience was stunned by the breadth of his knowledge, the scholarship of his references, and the totality of his support for the South. His decision was an iron-studded gauntlet flung into the teeth of the North. Its conclusions were so shocking that every one of the other eight justices issued his own decision, but on the big issues the vote was 7 to 2 supporting Taney.

His conclusions were bold and startling. No slave could ever be a citizen. In fact, no black, slave or not, could ever be a citizen. Slaves were property, just like mules and wagons, and the right to hold property must be protected. Then, in his Southern zeal to settle the slavery question once and for all, Taney threw in several opinions of his own, *obiter dicta* they were called, interesting conclusions but not justified by the data in the case at hand. They were inflammable: the Missouri Compromise of 1820, adjudicating which new states should be free of slavery, was unconstitutional; and even though a slave gained temporary freedom by running away to the North, if he ever returned to slave territory, he became once more a slave.

These judgments, so alien to the general drift of the nation in 1857, were harsh enough to arouse the fears of the Northern states, but Taney compounded his terrible error by inserting a protracted essay about the genesis of slavery, which did great damage. Taney never said that *he* believed what he was about to say; he was merely citing what the framers believed when they wrote the Constitution, but the phrases were so brutal that thousands of Northerners, upon hearing them, decided then and forever that since these were the opinions of the Court, any further compromise with the South was impossible:

> Negroes were not intended to be included under the word *citizens* and can, therefore, claim none of the rights and privileges of citizens. . . . They were considered as a subordinate and inferior class of beings who had been subjugated by the dominant race, and whether emancipated or not, yet remained subject to their authority, and had no rights or privileges but such as those who held the power might choose to grant them.

> They had been regarded as beings of an inferior order; and altogether unfit to associate

with the white race, either in social or political relations; and so far inferior that they had no rights which the white man was bound to respect; and that the negro might justly and lawfully be reduced to slavery for his benefit. He was bought and sold, and treated as an ordinary article of merchandise and traffic, whenever a profit could be made by it.

Another justice added:

The stigma of the black slave, of the deepest degradation, was fixed upon the whole race.

And then it became clear how Taney justified his basic decision: since the Founding Fathers in 1787 believed these things about black people, the judgment was fixed forever; blacks could neither obtain now nor expect in the future any relief in the courts. In 1787 the framers of the Constitution had considered them non-beings devoid of any rights, and so they must continue perpetually.

Hugh Starr, having just clarified his own thinking about slavery. and having freed his own, was appalled that the Supreme Court could issue such a document, for it lagged fifty years behind informed thinking, and he was not surprised when his fellow officers from the North scorned the Court's opinion. Even level-headed Benjamin Greer said: 'Your

Southern justices make it impossible for us Northern states to remain in a union to be governed by such laws,' and for several painful weeks young Starr remained apart from his friends, striving to find even a shred of justification for the *Dred Scott Decision*.

He found none. Just as his grandfather's Constitutional Convention had lacked the courage to grapple with the slave problem in its day, so this Supreme Court failed to provide the type of guidance necessary to preserve the Union. When his perplexity subsided, he sought out his friends and tried to probe their thinking, but a veil had dropped between North and South, and relationships at West Point were strained.

Said Starr one night, after trying in vain to talk with the Northerners: 'The Supreme Court agitates the nation, and the Army pacifies it. Something's topsy-turvy.' And the confusions deepened.

The frenzied presidential campaign of 1860 revealed just how chaotic conditions had become. The animosities of the *Dred Scott Decision* produced four major contestants for the presidency. Young officers from the Northern states had never heard of John Cabell Breckenridge and John Bell, the favorites of the South, while Hugh and his Southerners, although familiar with Senator Stephen Douglas, knew little of the lanky former congressman, this Lincoln. Both groups were astounded when Abraham Lincoln won on a strictly regional vote, and on the night the results were known, a brassy-voiced officer from Georgia shouted warning of what loomed ahead: 'Lincoln got not a single vote from the South! He's not my President!'

Now the wonderful camaraderie of the Point evaporated as one Southern officer after another quietly surrendered his commission in what he perceived as the Northern army, and slipped home to the Southern state which had always commanded his allegiance. Departing officers confided to their friends: 'If trouble comes, and I don't see how it can be avoided, I've got to be a South Carolina man.' It would not have been proper for secession to be openly discussed at the Point, but as the date for Lincoln's stormy inauguration approached, worried friends discussed their options in whispers, and Starr saw that the nation his ancestors had fought so diligently to create and preserve was destined to fracture along North-South lines.

Then came the real problem: But if war comes, what do I do? On the morning after he first dared to voice this question, three of his friends left the Point to return South and offer their services to their state militias, and Hugh narrowed his question: A choice between the Union and Virginia, what then? The problem was made more difficult when the commandant summoned him to share good news: 'Captain Starr, I have here your promotion to major in the Army of the United States. Congratulations.' Hugh accepted, but in doing so, realized that he was binding himself ever more strongly to the Union.

Alone in his quarters, he remembered the advice Jared Starr had given his son Simon in his deathbed letter in 1787: 'Fashion a strong new form of government but protect Virginia's interests.'

Ah, but what were 'Virginia's interests'? He had begun to think that the time might be at hand when Virginia should join with Massachusetts, New York and Pennsylvania as the four powerful states of the Union and forget sentimental and romantic attachments to the South: Sensible Virginians like my brother see that their interests are best protected by giving their slaves freedom, right now. They want no part of the *Dred Scott Decision*. But Virginia is tied to the other Southern states by bonds of iron, and so I suppose we must help them fight their battles defending slavery. Since Greer and the other Northerners will never allow slavery to move west, war becomes inescapable. And then what do I do?

In March 1861 he went on leave to his home in Virginia, where he spent happy days with his wife and children, son Malcolm and daughter Emily. He found his neighbors uneasy about the civil war that loomed, but none who even considered fighting on the Northern side. His brother, now the master of a prosperous plantation on which freed slaves worked effectively, summarized local thought: 'It will be war to defend a way of life. Virginia planters against Northern factory owners.' His brother always spoke as if Virginia alone would bear the military burden, but even though he disliked the arrogant way in which Carolina and Georgia men handled the slavery issue, he felt that Virginia must line up with them, and Hugh agreed.

Both the spring idyll in Virginia and the intellectual uncertainty about the forthcoming war vanished when shocking word reached the Starr plantation: 'President Lincoln offered Colonel Lee command of all Federal forces, and Lee refused. Said he respected the Union, but his heart was with Virginia.'

'What's it mean?' Hugh asked, and his informant said: 'Lee's to be general of the Southern armies.'

'Then it's war?'

'Don't see how it can be avoided.' That afternoon Hugh rode to Richmond, where he was commissioned Lieutenant Colonel Starr, Army of the Confederacy, and when the war came, he welcomed it.

During the next four years he served at Lee's right hand, sharing both the exciting early victories and the trailing defeats. His loyalty to Robert E. Lee duplicated Simon Starr's loyalty to Alexander Hamilton, and Lee in turn gave repeated evidence of his high regard for Starr's reliability, promoting him to full colonel, then to brigadier general.

Between battles, there were painful moments when it was clear that even Lee was beginning to wonder if the South could ever win against the vast Northern superiority in men and equipment, but more distressing were those night doubts which Hugh could share with no one: I wonder if the South deserves to win? I wonder if we aren't backing the wrong forces in history?

He could not believe that he and his brother were wrong in freeing their slaves, and when his personal servant Hannibal asked permission to accompany him on one campaign, he saw confirmation of what he had often suspected in the past: He's capable of anything, that Hannibal. But he did not go so far as to accept the abolitionist propaganda. 'Most of the Negroes aren't worth much,' he said, 'but the good ones can be exceptional.' Yet when he inspected the free village that his brother had established for the former Starr slaves, he found it at least as well tended as villages occupied by lower-class whites.

As the War Between the States ground painfully toward certain defeat for the South, General Starr felt contradictory and agonizing emotions: My heart bleeds for General Lee. Like him, I weep for Virginia. But I'm also glad the Union is to be preserved. Northern men like General Greer are too good to lose. And then a most powerful thought possessed him, clear as the sound of a bugle on the morning of battle: Twenty years from now you won't be able to tell South from North. In things that matter, that is.

Hugh Starr stood resolutely beside General Lee during the fatal last weeks of the Confederacy, participated in the surrender at Appomattox, and then turned his attention to mending the stricken fortunes of Virginia, and this brought our family right back into the heart of the Constitution, which had treated Hugh so poorly in its gross failure to solve the slavery problem at the time of *Dred Scott*.

In rapid-fire order the victorious Northern Congress passed three amendments, which should have gone into effect as early as 1820. The Thirteenth abolished slavery, the Fourteenth awarded blacks the civil rights that *Dred Scott* denied them, while the Fifteenth said simply that no citizen should be denied the right to vote because of 'race, color or previous condition of servitude.'

General Starr achieved notoriety, not always of a favorable kind, by standing forth as a Virginia defender of these amendments: 'Long overdue. About eighty years.' He visited various cities throughout the South, assuring men and women who were sometimes close to despair that the carpetbaggers from the North would soon be gone, that the disqualifications which dogged former Confederate leaders like himself would be lifted, and that devising new patterns for living with black folk would be the constructive task for the next two decades.

'That Virginia will rise again to the preeminent position she enjoyed in 1830, I have no doubt. We have the laws now and the men and women of ability. Let's get on with it.' In the evenings he met with veterans who wanted to know what it had been like serving with Robert E. Lee, and after describing this battle or that, he ended: 'We all have a chance to serve with him again. He's working to rebuild the South and we must assist him.'

Emily
Starr

1858–1932

EARLY SUNDAY MORNING our phone jangled. It was Zack: 'Can I come over?' and when he arrived from church he accepted a glass of cider and began questioning me: 'You got everything lined up? Your head screwed on tight?' When I assured him I'd been reviewing family records, he said: 'Good. I'm sure I can save your neck. I don't think they can lay a hand on you. Not in that uniform, with those family heroes and your own three or four tiers of medals.'

He concluded with a bit of advice: 'Take it easy today. Listen to Mozart. Stay relaxed. Because tomorrow you'll need all your smarts.' And he was about to leave me to my somnolence when Nancy broke in with a question which had begun to gnaw at her as she reviewed my family history.

'Tell me, Zack. You're a lawyer who understands these things. Why, in the entire Constitution that governs our nation and in all the reports of the debates, are women never once mentioned? Slaves are and mules and soldiers and judges, but never a woman. Were we considered of no significance in a new land which needed all the babies it could get?'

He sat down again, for her question interested him. 'Well,' he said, 'the men who wrote the Constitution were influenced by European law. They had to be. What other law did they know?'

'But why the indifference to women?'

'Because of French law, mostly. An ancient concept called *feme covert*—old idea, old spelling—denoted a *covered woman*, a married woman whose only legal rights were those under the protection of her husband. Out of the goodness of his heart, her all-wise, all-just husband with his superior judgment could be relied upon to look after her property, her money and her civil rights.'

'How generous,' Nancy said.

'The principle of *feme covert* surfaced at its ugliest when a loving husband claimed, and got, the right to manage the huge dowry a merchant's daughter often brought to their marriage. I believe a lot of wealthy wives died mysteriously in those circumstances.'

'Do you believe in the principle of *feme covert*?'

'No, but the fathers of the Constitution did, more or less.' He snapped his fingers as a completely new idea struck his agile mind: 'Never thought of it before. I read the other day that an outrageous number of the founders had two wives, and quite a few had three. In those days of miserable medicine, child-bearing women were expendable. A man *expected* to have two or three wives. They were different from men, obviously more fragile. Men had to look after them, make decisions for them.'

In her traditional way, Nancy now asked some abrupt questions: 'You'd sort of like it if the old days came back, wouldn't you?'

'When I lose a case to a brilliant woman lawyer, I sure do.'

'Why did you divorce Pamela?'

'She wanted to find herself. Runs a bookstore in Bethesda.'

'In other words, she didn't buy the legal theories of our Founding Fathers?'

'Don't make it too complex. She fell in love with the owner of the store, who borrowed a slug of money from her. She'll lose every nickel, as any man who inspected the guy's profit-and-loss statement could have predicted.' Somewhat edgy, he turned to me: 'I'll pick you up at eight tomorrow.'

Wanting to thank him for his generous help, and also to apologize for Nancy's bluntness, I accompanied him to his car, and in our driveway he gave me the encouragement he knew I needed: 'Things look real solid, Norm. Stay limber.'

When I returned to the house, I realized that staying loose wasn't going to be as easy as Zack had made it sound, because Nancy immediately confronted me: 'That talk about the attitude of the Founding Fathers toward women makes me more interested than ever in the grand old lady of your clan.' And we spent the next few hours discussing General Hugh Starr's gangling daughter.

The General had two children, a son, Malcolm, born two years before the *Dred Scott Decision*, and a daughter, Emily, born a year after. Malcolm, who became my great-grandfather, was an extremely stuffy type who went to Princeton and spent his vacations visiting one grand house after another in Philadelphia, Long Island and points north, looking for an heiress. He found none.

And then, miraculously, an heiress wealthier than any he had dared hope for came seeking him. General Benjamin Greer of the Vermont Rifles, who had performed so gallantly in support of General Ulysses S. Grant at Vicksburg, had come to Washington on one of his periodic visits, and, as always, he wanted to spend one evening with his old friend from West Point and Bleeding Kansas days. He and General

Starr, fortunately, had never faced each other in battle, but their careers were so similar, Greer as an aide to Grant, Starr with Lee, that they had much to talk about.

This meeting was unusual in that Greer brought with him his attractive niece Anne, daughter of his older brother, a man who had moved to New Hampshire after the war to start a textile mill, which had prospered wondrously. 'The other Greers,' Benjamin called them in public; in private he profited from their good fortune and, in gratitude, had helped his nephews and nieces see aspects of American life they might otherwise have missed.

'You'll like the Starrs,' he had coached Anne before their arrival in Washington. 'Solid people. One son, one daughter and a father that General Lee called "my faithful right arm." '

It was a tempestuous courtship—it seemed to the two generals that both the young people fell in love at the same instant—and it rocketed to a Washington marriage graced by generals, senators and a cadre of New England textile millionaires.

Anne was regal as she posed that week in a white outfit while young Sargent painted her. You can see her in the museum in Philadelphia, a woman of unforgettable beauty, but also of great austerity. Women of wealth are apt to be like that.

She was so magnificent—that's really the only word—that she quite overshadowed poor Emily, and the discrepancy was so visible that the General knew he wouldn't have an easy time finding a husband for his daughter. She was taller than he thought a woman should be, gaunter than required, and quite graceless in a gawky way. Of course, I never saw her, but the history books are filled with photographs of her, tall and militant, swinging her pocketbook at policemen or being carted away to one or another of the four jails that housed her.

That came later, of course, because in the late 1870s, all three members of her family—the General, Malcolm, Anne—were busy devising tricks to trap a young man. Apart from his house in Washington, the General had almost no funds, but Anne did, and the family exhibited an aura of wealth which attracted several young men who would otherwise never have looked at Emily, let alone court her. Warfare had made the General a good judge of men, while Anne had had her own experiences with fortune hunters, so between them they sent scattering several young fellows who would have brought Emily only grief.

They were not so lucky with a chap named Nicky Poland, who had acquired at Amherst a social polish to which Anne said 'he was not really entitled.' He had little money of his own, a vague kind of job in New York, and two good suits which he interchanged for maximum effect. He was such a charmer that in 1881, when Emily was twenty-three, he came frighteningly close to persuading her to elope with him to a town in Maryland that arranged swift marriages with no questions asked.

Emily, eager to take herself off the aging hands of

her father, and persuaded that young Nicky had sufficient funds to support her, was about to flee Washington for a life of happiness. However, she confided her plans to her sister-in-law, who required only a few minutes to summon a family conclave, to which Nicky was invited. There in a sunny room, tea and biscuits were served, with little silver spoons for the marmalade, a delicacy young Poland had not tasted before. General Starr, tall and straight and almost funereal in his bleak presentation of facts, informed Nicky that the two Starr men had practically no money, that Emily had less, and that they were all living off the generosity of Anne Greer Starr.

Before Poland could react to this appalling news, Anne made a little speech, which has come down in our family from father to daughter: 'Mr. Poland, what the General has just said is true. The obvious wealth in this family comes all from my father and me. Emily here has not a penny, nor will she ever get a penny if she elopes with you. Now, hadn't you better leave this house and Washington, taking this envelope with you?'

Anne never told anyone what was in that envelope, but if it was money, it was sufficient to get Nicky Poland out of the room and out of Washington, too.

Now, to save Emily's self-respect, the family felt it obligatory to find her a replacement, and since the two Starr men showed no skill at that task the burden fell on Anne, who brought to the Starr home one eligible young man after another, none of whom returned voluntarily, for at twenty-four, Emily was even less enticing.

'We must do something with your hair, Emmy,' Anne said. 'And you ought to smooth out your piano playing.' Brother Malcolm was more direct: 'Emmy, a girl with few graces has until her twenty-fifth birthday to get married. Anne has been most generous in helping you, but now you must help yourself.'

And that was when the Starrs first realized that in their Emily, they had a young woman quite out of the ordinary, because she said to her brother, within earshot of both Anne and the General; 'I've been thinking there might be more to a human life than being wife to someone who doesn't want me.'

Three gasps greeted this extraordinary assault on values, but since the revolutionary subject was now opened, Emily revealed the amazing turn her thinking had taken: 'In all the noble work the men of our family did, Declaration of Independence to the rebuilding after Appomattox, Father, the word *woman* is never once mentioned. Women were not declared free in 1776. They weren't mentioned once during the Convention. Grandfather Edmund never handed down a decision to protect or guide them. And the War Between the States was fought by men for men's reasons.'

'Emily!' the General cried, as if his honor had been impugned. 'The men of the South *revered* women . . .'

'If women had been consulted in that ridiculous affair, it would have ended in 1861.'

There was more, a whipping back and forth, laying bare ugly wounds that had not previously been ventilated, and at the conclusion, the General said: 'Emily, you talk like an enlightened woman bred in Massachusetts, and an uglier tribe was never born.'

Leaving her alone in the darkening room, the three retreated to the General's study, where they conducted a painful discussion on 'what to do with Emily,' and once again Anne volunteered to take draconian measures: 'She finds herself a husband within the year, or it's over.' Before anyone could react, she corrected herself: 'No, we must find her a husband within the year.'

That was how a shy, attractive man from Connecticut appeared at the Starr home. Philip Rawson was twenty-nine, unmarried and a distant cousin of the wealthy Greers. The money had not flowed his family's way, but Anne had intimated to Philip that if he found Emily interesting, he would also find his fortunes enhanced, considerably.

He proved to be such an amiable fellow that the Starrs were happy to have him as a guest. Emily, cognizant of the fact that Anne and Malcolm had gone far out of their way to find him, actually blossomed, to an extent that caused the General to confide to his son: 'I think our problems are solved.' But Malcolm warned: 'Only if she doesn't resume that nonsense she was talking.'

One night, while Emily was playing the piano for Philip, the other three Starrs held a council of war in the General's study, where Malcolm posed the question that had been worrying his father: 'If this Rawson is as acceptable as he seems, why hasn't he married long before this?' and Anne explained: 'I wrote to friends in Hartford to ask that same question.'

'And what did they say?'

'The Rawsons are even poorer than I thought. They had two daughters to marry off and there was nothing left for Philip. He makes such a pitiful living as a librarian that he felt he could not fairly ask any girl of good family to marry him.' She paused. 'I find him quite acceptable and we must pray that things go well.'

They did. He was enamored of books and introduced Emily to the richly textured works of William Dean Howells. At the end of three weeks, when it had been understood that he would leave, Anne asked him to stay on, and she extended her invitation in such a way that he now knew without question that they wanted him to consider an alliance with Emily. He accepted this invitation so graciously that Malcolm informed the General that night: 'I think we've solved Lady Emily's problem.'

And they might have, had not a tempestuous woman stormed into Washington at that moment. She was Kate Kedzie, widow of a Wyoming cattleman and the first woman in America to have voted in a general election. She had waited in a snowstorm to cast her ballot under the Territory of Wyoming's revolutionary law of 1869 granting woman suffrage. She was short, dynamic and darkened by the Western sun, but she was also intellectually mature, for she had attended college at Oberlin in Ohio, where she had developed her talents in music, physical education and oratory. Upon graduating, she did not return to her Indiana home to marry and raise children; she went instead to Chicago, where she found a job with a publisher and married his son, who had attended Yale. Together they moved west into Wyoming Territory, where they gambled their mutual savings on an enormous spread of almost barren land at six cents an acre. They thrived under frontier conditions, and when she surprised him by saying 'I think women should be allowed to vote,' he said 'Why not?' and the two formed the team which initiated and passed the legislation.

Having conquered the prejudices of her own area, Kate, as a widow, branched out into Colorado, where the miners rebuffed her with obscenities, and then into Kansas, where she was well received. Before she was fully aware of the transition, she had become a woman suffragist, working with great leaders like Susan B. Anthony and Elizabeth Cady Stanton in the apparently fruitless drive to alter the Constitution so that women could vote throughout the nation.

In frantic pursuit of that goal, she had come to Washington to persuade a reluctant Congress that an amendment was necessary, and at one of her first public meetings she made a soul-searing impression on Emily. Using every oratorical trick she had acquired at Oberlin, she finished in a low, pulsating voice:

'We are the forgotten people. We are the abused, the trampled upon, the ridiculed, because we are powerless. But, my friends, a storm is rising, and above it our voices will be heard. Justice, we cry! We demand justice! And . . . we shall . . . attain . . . it!'

Emily did not move forward to speak to her that night, nor on the two nights that followed, but Kate Kedzie was a clever woman. She had spotted reluctant converts before, so at the conclusion of her fourth stormy lecture she reached out, caught Emily by the wrist, and asked: 'Who are you, young woman?'

'I live here. Emily Starr.'

'Are you of my persuasion?'

'I think so.' And from that hesitant beginning, Emily became a suffragist who suspected that she might be entering upon a battle that could last the rest of her life. The Constitution must be changed so that all women could enjoy the political and property rights that Kate Kedzie had won for Wyoming in 1869.

Emily's introduction to the fray was dramatic, for on a June morning in 1886 her father choked on his breakfast eggs, and roared: 'Emily, what's this in the paper?' and there it was:

Among the speakers on behalf of what she claimed were 'long-delayed women's rights' was the daughter of General Hugh Starr, who said in a voice that could scarcely be heard: 'We shall fight for the ballot in every known venue until Congress offers the states a chance to vote on an amendment.' Loud boos greeted the challenge, but Miss Starr held her own.

The General was a formidable man, fifty-three years old and in full possession of his considerable force. Should a new war erupt on Monday, he would be ready to ride forth on Tuesday, so he was more than ready to punish his daughter's assault on decency: 'Did you parade yourself in public?'

'Yes,' spoken firmly.

'And you presumed to advise Congress?'

'I did.'

A torrent of abuse followed, scathing in its denunciation of women who wanted to be men and contemptuous of the idea that they might want the vote or know what to do with it if they got it: 'Have you ever heard that splendid chain of words invented in Germany not long ago? *Kaiser, Kirche, Kinder, Küche.* That's what women really want. Obedience to the ruler. Faithfulness to the church. Care of the children. And supervision of the kitchen and home.'

Emily had hoped to avoid confrontation with her father, but she was so imbued with the daring ideas of Kate Kedzie that she simply could not remain silent: 'I think that if our form of government has errors, they must be corrected—'

'Errors? And who are you to determine error?'

'If half the population is denied participation—'

'Participation? You women run the home, highest calling in Christendom. What more do you want? A soldier's uniform and a gun?'

He was so agitated that he dispatched one of his daughter-in-law's servants to fetch Anne and Malcolm, and when they appeared in dressing gowns, for they rose late, a triumvirate was formed, three people who would oppose Emily for the rest of her life: General Hugh in the middle, stern and forbidding; brother Malcolm on his left, pallid but always willing to preach; sister-in-law Anne on the General's right, cool and able and formidable.

The General spoke first: 'Our Emily has disgraced herself. Acting up in public. Wants women to be soldiers.' He ranted for nearly five minutes, ridiculing his daughter's aspirations and lampooning her presumptions: 'Suffragists? Is there an uglier word in the language? I would march to the shore and swim away if my country ever encouraged women to leave the sanctuary of the home and dirty themselves in cheap politics.'

He looked to his son for confirmation, but Malcolm, like many indecisive men who have married women wealthier and brighter than themselves, merely nodded and deferred to his wife.

Now another phenomenon of this tense period in American life began to manifest itself. Anne Greer, a woman of privilege with six servants, became a vigorous foe of everything that her sister-in-law Emily was fighting for: 'The General is right. Woman's place is within the chapel of the home, tending it, making it a haven, providing a refuge from the busy cares of the world . . .' On and on she went about the glories of homemaking, despite the fact that she never performed any of these tasks; her servants did.

But her first outburst was so effective, so filled with cherishable imagery that Emily thought: She'll be more dangerous than the men. And that would be true, for without waiting for a chastised Emily to disappear, Anne said: 'The thing to do is get Philip Rawson down here immediately, and you marry him, Emily, because he's your last chance.'

Philip, summoned by telegraph, arrived on the first train, and his courtship was both proper and forceful. It was obvious that he had grown to like Emily and dislike the prospect of endless years in a Connecticut library. On her part, Emily appreciated what a decent young man he was and how, on the assured income that Anne promised, they could have a meaningful life together. Malcolm, supervising the strange wooing, reported to his co-conspirators: 'I think it's settled. We can be damned grateful.'

But now Kate Kedzie blustered back into town for her next shouting match with congressmen, and when Emily unwisely invited her home for tea, the other four very tense Starrs, counting Philip Rawson as one soon to be, met uneasily with the type of new woman they had not previously encountered. It was not a pleasant afternoon, especially when Kate told the three men, hoping to enlist their support: 'It was actually my husband who got the movement started in Wyoming.'

'I should think,' the General snapped, 'that men of any significance in their community would unite to oppose this foolishness,' to which Kate replied with a smile: 'But isn't the real foolishness for men to suppose that they can continue to hold in bondage fifty percent of our population?'

Here Malcolm broke in with a beautiful non sequitur that Nancy and I always chuckle about when we remember it: 'Slavery was the real bondage, and my father gave his slaves their freedom even before the war started.'

From there the afternoon degenerated, with Anne making perhaps the most ominous and revealing comment: 'You must be aware, Mrs. Kedzie, that women of breeding will oppose the ugly things you're trying to do, and oppose you with skill.'

'You always have,' Kate said icily, and warfare between these two was declared.

Kate won the first engagement, because when the tea ended, Emily boldly left her family and accompanied the Wyoming suffragist to a public meeting, where she not only spoke with some effectiveness but also tussled with the police and went to jail.

After Anne gave Malcolm the money to pay her bail, the General took Emily into his study, and said fiercely: 'Young lady, this has to stop,' and she, hoping to remain friends with him, asked pleadingly: 'Father, why were you so generous in defending black slaves? I've always been proud of you for that. But now the next reform comes along and you're dead set against us.'

He saw no anomaly. 'Blacks like Hannibal knew their place and I was proud to help them. Everyone has a proper place, and women should not be seen ranting and raving in the streets or lecturing United States senators.'

He felt so strongly about this that he convened a no-nonsense family meeting in which he read the riot act, with Anne delivering the crucial blows: 'Emily, if you ever repeat this disgraceful behavior, your father and your brother will not want you to remain in this house. It's too embarrassing.' Then she turned to Librarian Rawson, who had earlier been informed that the promised dowry for Emily would not be forthcoming if she persisted in her shameful ways. Realizing that without such a dowry, a Rawson-Starr marriage would be impossible, he told Emily in front of the others: 'No man can retain his self-respect if a wife acts up in public. Real women don't want the vote. They want the security of a good home . . . where they are in command.'

Emily felt dizzy and was afraid she was going to be sick. The forces arrayed against her were too powerful. Her father was remorseless; Anne was too clever; and Philip, the person she had begun to feel might be her partner, had turned traitor. Ignoring the others, she stepped before him and said: 'There's always been a great wrong in this nation and I must try to correct it. I'm sorry, Philip,' and the threatened sickness passed as she left her family and her intended husband.

Nancy and I have a scrapbook which someone in our family put together. It shows in ugly images Emily Starr's turbulent years at the change of centuries, and often Nancy has tears in her eyes as we see this procession of determined women in their long black skirts being attacked and reviled and even spat upon. Nancy says: 'I wouldn't have had the courage,' and I tell her honestly: 'I might have reacted just like Malcolm or Rawson. I wouldn't have been prepared for this.'

In the scrapbook there is one newspaper clipping which summarizes the opposition my great-aunt faced:

> Who opposes these Amazon women? Honest politicians resist because they can't guess how women will vote, dishonest ones because they fear women might support reform movements. The brewing interests pour in vast sums of money lest their saloons be closed, and the South is solidly opposed for fear of what black women might do if they ever voted. Protestant churches which accept St. Paul's fulminations against women fight tooth and nail, and recently Cardinal Gibbons enrolled his Catholics against them. But the most effective foe is the wealthy woman like Anne Starr who testifies that real women don't want or need these so-called rights.

When I pointed to this formidable list of enemies, Nancy pushed the scrapbook away, looked up in disbelief, and asked: 'Norman, how did she muster the courage to fight such an array?'

I shared a conclusion taught me by my mother, who would, in her day, fight her own battle for a worthy cause: 'All Starr children were reared to believe that they had a family stake in the Constitution. Emily saw the document as a national legacy which needed her protection. She said once: "If Jared and Simon gave their lives defending freedom, the least we can do in our generation is continue their work." Her battle came naturally . . . inevitably.'

It was someone not favorable to suffragists who devised the idea of inviting the two Starr women to debate, first in Washington, then in the major cities, and at first Anne, always gracious and condescending, simply swamped ungainly Emily, whose voice tended to become rasping as the evening progressed. Anne had one trick which delighted audiences and won them to her side:

> 'I have here in my hand a copy of the noble speech delivered on the floor of the Senate by one of our greatest political leaders, George Vest of Missouri: "For my part I want when I go home—when I turn from the arena where

man contends with man for what we call the prizes of this paltry world—I want to go back, not to the embrace of some female ward politician, but to the earnest, loving look and touch of a true woman. I want to go back to the jurisdiction of the wife, the mother; and instead of a lecture upon finance or the tariff, or upon the construction of the Constitution, I want those blessed loving details of domestic life and domestic love." '

Invariably when Anne read this, standing erect and looking exactly like the kind of wife the senator had been describing, much of the audience broke into cheers, and Emily sometimes had difficulty getting them to listen to her.

But Kate Kedzie was a fighting woman, and one night when she was in the audience listening to Anne annihilate Emily, a fugitive idea popped into her head, and she spent the next morning in the Boston Public Library. That night the rejuvenation of Emily Starr and her crusade began, for when Anne started reading Senator Vest's oration on the proper role of women, Emily leaned forward, attracted attention to herself, and nodded warmly as the eight minutes of purple prose soared to its conclusion that women wanted nothing more than what men generously allowed them.

When Anne finished, to the usual applause, Emily went over, shook her hand as if she had surrendered the debate, then strode to the podium in forceful steps, and told the audience: 'Like you, I was enchanted by Senator Vest's ringing advice on how women ought to behave. He says he doesn't want us to be worrying about the Constitution. Well, you know by now that I do worry about it, a great deal, and I wonder who is the best judge of what women want from the Constitution, Senator Vest or me?'

Then, imitating the way in which Anne produced Vest's speech on women, she unfolded a paper and proceeded to read another of that same senator's famous orations:

' "The one absolutely unselfish friend that man can have in this selfish world, the one that never deserts him, the one that never proves ungrateful or treacherous, is his dog. A man's dog stands by him in prosperity and in poverty, in health and sickness. He guards the sleep of his pauper master as if he were a prince. When all other friends desert, he remains." '

And on and on. As she poured forth Vest's impassioned defense of dogs, listeners had to realize that he had said much the same about women. Here and there people began to chuckle and then burst into guffaws, for the two speeches sounded identical. Emily's punch line was devastating: 'Senator Vest seems confused as to whether he wants a woman or a puppy dog. I want women who have an interest in their

Constitution and who want to amend it so that justice is given to all.' Now the same audience that had applauded Vest's first speech on women, cheered with real animation Emily's adroit use of his second speech on his affection and respect for dogs.

Unwisely, Anne tried to continue using the Vest speech on women in Boston and Hartford, but when Emily practically laughed her off the stage with his oration on dogs, she stopped. But Kate Kedzie would not let her escape, and in Pittsburgh, when Anne avoided the Vest speech, Emily said remorselessly:

> 'Two weeks ago my opponent drew much laughter when she read a senator's speech ridiculing what we women want. But when I found another speech by the same man proving how ridiculous his words were and how empty, she stopped using hers. Well, because you've read about this in the papers, I'm going to read you both speeches, hers and mine, and you'll see that our opponents can't tell the difference between real women and dogs.'

She read in tones of such withering scorn, revealing Anne Starr as a pampered woman of curious persuasions, that the enmity between them became mortal. Never again would Anne allow herself to be in the same house or room or debating hall with her sister-in-law. This meant that Emily was now completely cut off from her family, but whenever she went to jail, the papers still referred to her as the daughter of Confederate General Hugh Starr, devoted right-hand man to General Lee.

In early 1918 it looked as if Kate and her indomitable women might gain their victory in Washington just as our male troops were gaining theirs in Europe, but women like Emily Starr underestimated the venom with which leading American politicians would fight against them. William Borah of Idaho thundered, so did William Bankhead of Alabama, James Wadsworth of New York, Henry Cabot Lodge of Massachusetts and Pitchfork Ben Tillman of South Carolina, before he died. Assured of their numbers, these implacable foes grudgingly allowed a Senate vote in early February 1919, and the women lost by one.

Emily, now sixty-one, was so distraught by the defeat and so infuriated by the opposition of religious leaders who trivialized her crusade that she was trapped into a pathetic error which alienated her friends and destroyed her future effectiveness in the movement. When a leading churchman exulted: 'The Senate rejection of women's suffrage proves that the devout people of the United States still adhere to the Christian principles of our Constitution,' she sat in fury reviewing the notes of her great-grandfather Simon Starr and the journal of James Madison. Satisfied as to the truth, she published a pamphlet whose opening sentences made cautious women cringe:

It is time we realized that religion had practically nothing to do with the drafting of our

Constitution. Practical human beings wrote it, and since they were subject to every frailty that you and I suffer, if they committed error or oversight, it ought to be corrected.

The outcry was tremendous, but those who did not instantly dismiss the pamphlet as atheism learned something about the genesis of their country:

It is wrong for Reverend Waterson to depict the framers as praying for divine guidance and seeking God's counsel before composing our Constitution. True, the delegates were religious men and most attended church on the weekends, but once they convened in the meeting hall, they did not allow religious matters to enter their deliberations. Since three of the delegates had been trained for the ministry, religious values must have been taken into consideration, but look what happened to these three would-be clergymen. Hugh Williamson of North Carolina became licensed as a Presbyterian clergyman, but he quit early to become a scientist. Abraham Baldwin of Georgia, after graduating from Yale, was asked to stay on as its chaplain and later was offered a professorship of divinity, but chose instead to become a lawyer-politician. And the great James Madison studied for the ministry at Princeton, found he had no vocation, and turned to politics.

Not one of these men, or any other, sponsored religious positions in the Convention. However, at the close of one long day of angry debate, Dr. Franklin proposed that tempers might be softened if each session opened with prayer. His suggestion brought little support and was not even brought to a vote, but Madison's cryptic notes suggest that it occasioned a lot of parliamentary maneuvering before it was allowed to die. Curiously, it was effectively disposed of by Clergyman Williamson, who observed dryly that the matter should be dropped because the Convention had no funds to pay a minister.

A careful reading of documents circulating at the time proves that whereas the delegates were in general a religious group, they were terrified of the religious intolerances they had read about in history or observed in their own colonies. They resisted every attempt to insert in their Constitution any flaming reaffirmations of human rights or religious freedoms, and in the end their only reference to religion was the brief, sharp warning that comes at the very end of the substantial part of the law: 'No religious test shall ever be required as a qualification to any office or public trust under the United States.'

But in their austerity the delegates under-estimated the essentially religious nature of the American people. Families went to church. Their children were baptized. Clergymen were respected. Public prayer was common, and there was general obedience to an inherited ethic. However, the infant United States was not a Christian nation and the founders did not so describe it, but it was a nation dedicated to Judeo-Christian principles. Therefore, when a powerful surge of opinion demanded a Bill of Rights, Congress acquiesced, and if it had not, the Constitution would probably have been rejected.

But even in the famous First Amendment, the statement regarding religion is negative and protective: 'Congress shall make no law respecting an establishment of religion,' and not until that safeguard from oppression had been established did the positive promise come: 'or prohibiting the free exercise thereof.' The framers were tough-minded practical men who respected religion for the moral balance it contributes to society, but the structure of government they devised was pragmatic rather than religious, and it worked. Now, as pragmatists like our forefathers, we women want to ensure that it still works.

When she was abused from all sides for being an atheist, Emily retaliated with a second pamphlet even more incendiary than the first, for now she argued that all religion was notoriously anti-woman. She cited pagan rites, which sacrificed women to pagan gods; the Jewish religion, which segregated women infamously; the Catholics, who denied women any serious role in the governance of their church; the Puritan religions of New England, which did not protest when their older women were hanged as witches; and she closed with a blast against the Mormons, who denigrated women, and the Quakers, who separated them from men in their Philadelphia meeting houses. She concluded her diatribe with a plea and a threat:

> Please cleanse your faiths of antique practices which deny women full partnership, because the women of America will no longer kowtow to the fulminations of St. Paul.

An outcast, she was advised not to be present in the Senate chamber on 4 June 1919 when the final vote was taken, so she did not participate in the joyous applause when women finally won. After a century of struggle, Congress had passed a bill which did not actually establish suffrage; it merely invited the individual states to ratify or reject a simple one-sentence amendment: 'The right of citizens of the United States to vote shall not be denied or abridged by the United States or by any State on account of sex.'

That night there was celebration, to which Emily was not invited, but early next morning she sought out Kate, and warned: 'Now our real fight begins. We've got to persuade three-fourths of the states to ratify. That's thirty-six. And the enemy will oppose us with greater fury than ever before.'

She was correct. The fight was brutal, with many of America's most generous and thoughtful men vilifying women who sought to soil themselves with the vote. Her friends in the movement told her bluntly: 'Stay under cover. With the charges of atheism, you do us more harm than good.' So for the remainder of 1919 and early 1920 she traveled back roads, avoiding public meetings and newspaper people, meeting quietly with old friends who needed her fortifying strength: 'Keep working. We must have thirty-six, but we can count on only thirty-three.'

Finally, it all depended on what happened in Tennessee, where in a small hill town a twenty-four-year-old member of the state's lower house, one Harry Burn, was under extreme pressure. His mother preached: 'Vote for the women, son. Only decent thing to do,' but the clergymen and the business leaders hammered: 'Don't disgrace yourself with a vote for those Amazons.'

Emily, whose calculations convinced her that the

vote might hinge on Burn, quietly stopped by his home to talk with mother and son. With him, she accomplished nothing: 'Ever'body tells me it ain't right for women to mix theirselves in politics.' But with Mrs. Burn, she had a better reception, and long into the night the two women talked. Next morning, when Harry set out for the capital, his mother told him: 'Don't forget to be a good boy. Vote for suffrage and don't keep them in doubt.'

When Emily reached the capital on the eve of the final vote, she was horrified to learn that the opposition had brought in so much free liquor that the entire legislature was blind-drunk and no vote could be taken. That night she slept in a rooming house where no one knew her, and the hours were endless: Oh no, not back to the beginning again. Fight it once more through the House? Once more through the Senate? I wouldn't have the strength.

Next day the sobered Tennessee Senate ratified the amendment, and now all focused on the lower house, where the opposition had what they judged to be enough votes to defeat the women one last time: 'Harry Burn is with us. Eddie took care of him.'

When Emily slipped into the hall where the legislators would meet, a suffragist recognized her, and whispered: 'We think it's going to be forty-eight to forty-eight. We've lost.'

'How about Harry Burn?'

The woman looked at her list, and said: 'He went over to the other side. Damn.'

In the breathless counting of votes, there were two

surprises. The women lost one vote but picked up two, and if Harry Burn voted with them, they would win. If not, it would be the predicted tie, which would mean that they had lost yet again.

All turned to stare at the young fellow who had been pressured by both sides. When the clerk called for his vote, he replied in a whisper 'Yea,' and it seemed as if the entire capital burst into curses and cheers. The Constitution of the United States had been modified in accordance with orderly procedures laid down a hundred and thirty-three years before.

That night Emily Starr, an outcast from her family, her friends and even her own group of crusaders, stood in the smallest bedroom of the little Tennessee boardinghouse, still clad in her long black dress and outmoded hat, experiencing the terrible loneliness that can overtake good people when they have won a significant battle. She felt no sense of triumph. An involuntary cry escaped: 'Oh, Philip! It needn't have been so.'

Then she stiffened, averted her eyes from the small mirror, and said: 'It was wrong and it had to be set right.'

Richard
Starr

1890–1954

SINCE my grandfather died when I was only three, I can scarcely claim that I knew him, but I do remember his coming to our house and bouncing me on his knee. He was tall and thin, and cranky, except to me, and he smelled of tobacco. I certainly remember his funeral. It was a cold, misty day, and someone said something I can still recall: 'The day is as mean as the man.'

He had not always been that way, and some of

the stories about him that were repeated in our home bespoke a kindlier young man. But financial reverses in the Great Depression embittered him, and it was his sour behavior in his later years which dominated the stories.

In the early days of his marriage he was well-to-do or even rich, the result of an inheritance from his mother, one of the Greer textile family of New Hampshire, so he never really had to work. He was in what they called at the time 'investments,' and since he was neither brilliant nor particularly adept at managing money, his adventures turned out poorly, and the Crash of 1929 damaged him.

It was then that he developed the great passion of his life, for he became known as 'the man who hated Roosevelt.' When I was a boy the letters F.D.R. were anathema in our house, for my grandfather had said that he had tried to turn America into a Communist state.

'It began with those damn-fool amendments,' he stormed. 'Why meddle with the Constitution? Like they say, "Why fix it if it ain't broke?" '

He described the Seventeenth Amendment, which called for the election of senators by popular vote, a tragic mistake: 'In the old days you had men of property and breeding in the state legislatures, and they could be depended upon to appoint men like themselves, men of substance, to the Senate.' He believed that to allow the general public to determine the character of our upper chamber was the first step toward revolution: 'Just watch what comes out of the

Senate now,' and when the first laws were enacted, he went about crying: 'The rot has begun!'

His opinion of the Nineteenth Amendment was sulfurous: 'The brightest day in the history of the Starr family was when my grandfather, General Hugh, cast his lot with Robert E. Lee . . . the darkest was when that crazy daughter of his, Aunt Emily, started working for women's suffrage.' Of course, he inherited his impression of the infamous Emily from his mother, Anne Greer, whose scornful memory of her sister-in-law intensified as the years passed. She once told my grandfather of that hideous night when Emily had made a fool of her: 'She mimicked me, she laughed at me, humiliated me in every way, and I never spoke to her again as long as she lived. She was a dreadful person and she introduced alien ideas into American politics.'

But my grandfather's harshest abuse fell on the Sixteenth Amendment, which authorized the collection of income taxes: 'If that damn thing hadn't been passed, you'd be a rich man, Thomas,' he used to tell my father, overlooking the fact that his own unskilled investing had been the cause of his misfortune, not the income tax.

What gave him special cause for remorse was the fact that each of these amendments had been passed in his lifetime: 'If I'd been paying attention, maybe I could have stopped them. Maybe we patriots were caught napping.' Repeatedly he lectured my father on this point: 'Thomas, never let them meddle with the Constitution. It's perfect as it is,' and he cited the nonsense over how the Eighteenth Amendment tried to stop drinking: 'We let a lot of do-good women and teary-eyed ministers inflict it on us, and as soon as it came into effect, every sensible person knew it was a monstrous mistake that had to be corrected. Thank God, in due time men like me were able to get rid of it, but it should never have been sneaked into the Constitution in the first place.'

Before I discuss the event which gave my grandfather what he interpreted as a personal victory, I must explain just how deep his loathing of President Roosevelt went. In 1944, when the Twenty-seventh Division was removed from Saipan under humiliating circumstances, my father, Lieutenant Colonel Thomas Starr, lost a leg in the fracas and won himself the Congressional Medal of Honor, than which there is none higher. Grandfather, ecstatic to know that another Starr had behaved with honor, drove about Washington and northern Virginia telling everyone about Tom's heroism.

He was invited, of course, to the White House to share in his son's glory when the medal was presented, but when he realized that the conferring would be done by President Roosevelt, he refused to go: 'Any medal that son-of-a-bitch touched would be contaminated.' And when my father brought it home, Grandfather wouldn't touch it. But he did like to point to it when strangers dropped by.

In 1933 and '34, Grandfather had an especially bad time, for it was in those bleak years, when it looked as if our nation might fall apart, that F.D.R. initiated his radical reforms. Were such swift changes necessary to save our society? Who knows? Had I been living then, I think I might have supported the innovations, but who knows?

Grandfather knew: 'Roosevelt is a Communist. He's a worse dictator than Mussolini.' At one point he bellowed: 'Someone should shoot that Commie,' but Grandmother warned him: 'You say that where people can hear you, you'll go to jail.' If he did temper his public threats, he never relaxed his private hatred, and what he seemed to object to most was the intrusive way in which the regulations of Roosevelt's N.R.A. impinged on his life: 'National Recovery Act! Leave things alone, they'll take care of themselves. Meddling into everything, this is dictatorship at its worst.'

There was a popular song at the time, a silly jingle, 'Sam, You Made the Pants Too Long,' and one morning Grandfather saw this crazy headline in his newspaper:

Sam, You Can Make the Pants Longer or Shorter but You Better Not Charge More Than $2.50

'My God,' Grandfather shouted, slamming his paper to the floor. 'Now he's interfering in the work of tailors.'

And then, in his moments of apparent defeat, came triumph. It was a Supreme Court decision handed down in 1935 during the depth of the Depression, and it bore the curious title *Schecter Poultry Corporation* v. *United States*, and Grandfather claimed: 'It's the greatest case in the history of the United States. Saved this nation.' And in later years I've found others who felt somewhat the same.

The facts were clear. N.R.A. officials appointed by Roosevelt, not Congress, had issued a regulation, not a legally passed law, saying that you could not move sick chickens from one state to sell in another. The Schecter people found the order somehow oppressive and refused to obey. They continued to move chickens, well or sick, from New Jersey and into New York, so they had to be arrested. The case went to the Supreme Court, which declared 9 to 0 that the whole N.R.A. was unconstitutional in that it allowed the President to enact law, rather than Congress.

Well, when I first heard this story about Grandfather, I could understand little and I suspected my parents might have the facts garbled, but when I later learned the interpretation Grandfather gave the case, I tended to agree with him. He went about Virginia telling everyone: 'Roosevelt was a dictator, make no mistake about that, and the N.R.A. was his trick for fashioning chains of steel about our necks. Now, the history of the world is filled with cases in which dictators have used a temporary crisis to install illegal, crisis legislation. "The times demand it," they bellow, but mark my words, when the crisis ends, the dictators never leave office. They hang around until they destroy their countries.

'The miracle of the United States, we've just had

our dictator, a dreadful man, but when the crisis was over we had an agency, put in place more than a century before, which could say: "Crisis is over. Hand back the reins. We play by the rules again." Read about Cromwell in England. He came in just like Roosevelt, had many of the same kinds of laws. To get rid of him, they had to have a civil war. We did it with our Supreme Court.'

Roosevelt, outraged by the Schecter decision, which struck at his effort to restore the nation's economy, retaliated petulantly. He tried to pack the Supreme Court with additional judges guaranteed to vote his way, and when Grandfather heard of this plot he went berserk. An old man, still living in Virginia when I went off to West Point, told me: 'Your grandfather, always a patriot, assembled a group of us who knew something about politics, and we toured the South lambasting F.D.R. as a dictator and calling for impeachment. Your grandfather was especially effective, for he could shout at the crowds: "My ancestors signed the Declaration of Independence and helped write the Constitution and fought at the right hand of Robert E. Lee." The crowds cheered, believe me. And then he shouted: "We must defend the Constitution as written and stop Roosevelt in his tracks!" But when we talked late at night as we drove on to the next town, I found that your grandfather was pretty picky about how much of the Constitution he was willing to defend. He was happy with only the first part. He wasn't too keen on the Bill of Rights, he distrusted the Fourteenth and Fifteenth Amendments, which gave the colored folk more rights than they needed, and he positively loathed the Sixteenth, Seventeenth and Nineteenth. But with the help of a lot of others, we defeated Roosevelt's plan and saved the nation.'

Our family has clippings of the time Grandfather hit the headlines in a big way. His wife, that is, my grandmother, was a minor official in the Daughters of the American Revolution, and when someone that Grandfather called 'a misguided do-gooder and weeping heart' arranged for the splendid singer Marian Anderson to give a concert in Constitution Hall, my grandmother, who considered the Hall her property, canceled the permission on the grounds that 'it would be highly improper for a Negress to appear in such a hallowed place.' When public outrage exploded, Grandfather leaped to his wife's side, with a pronouncement which hit newspapers and radios across the nation: 'Constitution Hall is sacred to the memory of those patriots who wrote the Constitution and their descendants, and so far as I know, there were no Negroes in that Convention.'

And finally, my favorite story about the crusty old gentleman. He was born on 12 April 1890, and on that date in 1945— But let my father tell the story, since he was there: 'Proud of the way I was learning to manipulate my new leg, I was in the garden when I heard the kitchen radio announce that F.D.R. had died. Hobbling to my father's study, I cried: "Dad, have you heard? F.D.R. just died!"

'He waved me away: "You're teasing. Just saying that to make me feel good on my birthday." '

Rachel
Denham
Starr

1928–

ONE OF THE JOYS of my life has been that my wife, Nancy, gets on so amiably with my mother, Rachel Starr. Of course, this hasn't been difficult, because my wife has good sense and my mother by herself would be justification for the Nineteenth Amendment, which gave women the vote. She's one of the all-time winners.

On Sundays it was our custom for Nancy to leave our place in midafternoon, go over to my mother's, and help prepare a cold supper which all four of us would share at seven. I encouraged this because I found constant joy in talking with both my father and my mother.

So I was alone Sunday afternoon when Zack barged in without phoning first. He was obviously agitated, and quickly told me why: 'Norman, I've been with the big brains of our profession all yesterday afternoon and this morning, and they all think the situation is so clear that it presents no alternative.' He rose, walked about the room, and came to rest standing over me like an irate father: 'I said, they all said, there's no escape.'

'What's that mean?'

He walked some more, cleared his throat, then drew up a chair so that he could sit opposite me and very close: 'Norman, you aren't going to like this, but tomorrow morning you'll have to take the Fifth to protect yourself against incriminating yourself.'

I felt dizzy. From the days of the Kefauver Committee, which coincided with my birth, our family had scorned the criminals and spies and shifty ones who 'took the Fifth,' and one of my earliest memories is of my irascible grandfather shouting: 'Only thieves and crooks take the Fifth, so anyone who does should be shot.' I could not imagine any Starr in the past taking it, and for me to stand up in public and do so was unthinkable.

'No way I can take the Fifth,' I said.

I'm sure Zack must have known how I would react, but since he did try to persuade me, we sat in grim silence, neither knowing what to say next. At this moment Nancy returned to fetch something from the kitchen that my mother needed, and as soon as she saw us she cried: 'You two look like the hearse just passed,' and it was Zack who blurted out: 'It did. I just advised Norman that tomorrow in the Senate hearing he must take the Fifth.'

She stood stock-still, framed in the doorway, her pugnacious little chin pointed upward as always, and then she asked a totally unexpected question: 'Will they have whole batteries of television cameras, Zack?' And he replied: 'They will.'

She remained in the doorway, wreathed in sunlight, and I could not guess what she might say next, for she really knew only three things about my work. I was not involved with Iran. I was up to my neck in Nicaragua. And although I was under the command of Rear Admiral John Poindexter, I'd had only minimal contact with Colonel Oliver North. But what exactly I had done, and how much legal danger I might be in, she did not know, nor did any civilian, not even Vice-President Bush, for whose drug task force I had performed various lawful assignments that were on the public record and to the public benefit.

But she had strong opinions, this young housewife and community helper, and I could see that she was about to voice them: 'This nation has watched a Navy admiral take the Fifth, an Air Force general take the Fifth, and a Marine colonel. And they're fed up. If one more military man stands there and takes the

Fifth, it would sicken them. I do not want my husband to be the hero who finally makes them throw up.'

Zack, having expected such a rejection from me, was not surprised at my wife's outrage, but he knew how to deal with it: 'Nancy, sit down and stop the heroics. Your husband can go to prison if we don't handle this right, and by *we*, I mean all of us, you included. Now shut up and listen.'

From his papers he extracted his copy of the Fifth Amendment: '. . . *nor shall any person be subject for the same offense to be twice put in jeopardy of life or limb; nor shall be compelled in any criminal case to be a witness against himself* . . . It's there to protect everyone, innocent and guilty, from what governments used to do to extract testimony.' And in solemn tones he described the kinds of extracting of information that used to occur: the cutting off of ears, the dislocation of limbs on the rack, the hot oil in the ear, the incarceration in a cell too cramped to permit standing or sleeping. 'One of the noblest provisions in the Bill of Rights is the Fifth Amendment. And your husband is exactly the kind of person it was intended to protect.'

Stunned by the force of Zack's description of what trials used to be, even in Colonial America, Nancy took the chair he indicated, and asked: 'So he gets on the stand like all our other military heroes and crybabies?'

'No,' Zack said patiently, 'he protects himself, as

Simon Starr's Constitution invites him to . . . no, wants him to.'

'And then he begs the Senate Committee to grant him immunity?'

'Not beg. But I will certainly seek it for him . . . and get it!'

'Then what?'

'Well, he's supposed to tell all he knows, assist the committee.'

'You mean rat on his associates?' Nancy has the habit of reducing evasions to basics, and Zack did not like what he heard.

'Now you must understand . . .' he fumbled.

Nancy cut him short. Folding her hands in her lap and smiling warmly, she said: 'Zack, you've known us a long time without really knowing us. It's clear you don't understand Norman and me. He will not evade responsibility, never. And if facing up to the truth gets him in trouble, I can always go back to that data-processing I did when we got married. So if you think my husband, to save his own neck, would . . .'

It was a brave speech, but it did not impress Zack. He was a fighting redhead and he had coddled us long enough. Standing over us, he said: 'Yesterday morning, before I had the all-day session with our top lawyers, who know more about Washington than I ever will, I was one kind of guy and you were two ordinary people. Well, compadres, that's changed.'

'How?' Nancy asked, always ready for a fight.

'Because at the meeting this morning a man from

one of the top law firms informed us that he had certain proof that the Senate panel had someone who was going to blab about an affair in Nicaragua . . . maybe just over the border in Honduras, called Tres Toros.'

I remained perfectly calm, but both Zack and Nancy had to see that my knuckles had whitened. To Zack it was what he had expected, but to Nancy it was like a fire bell clanging at night. It terrified her, and suddenly the pugnacious battler became a trembling wife eager to protect her husband. She did not ask what Tres Toros was or what it signified; in a low voice she asked: 'What are we to do, Zack?'

He smiled at her as if he loved her, and said: 'We stay calm, all of us. Your husband takes the Fifth, and for one very good reason that supersedes all others.' And here his voice rose almost to a shout: 'To save his goddamned ass.' Then he sat down, wiped his forehead, and said quietly: 'There is no other way, Nancy. And with luck, I think I can bring this off. But Norman and I must have your support.'

I shivered, because when he had talked with me only that morning, he had said: 'I'm sure I can save your neck.' But after Nancy's outburst and the surfacing of the Tres Toros, his boast had been downgraded to: 'I think I can . . .'

It was a chastened pair of Starrs who drove to my parents' home for Sunday-night supper. Since Nancy was driving, I sat hunched in the shotgun seat pondering gloomily the things that faced me tomorrow. We rode in silence, through snow-plowed streets, for this was the time of year when Eastern states and especially Washington were hit by tremendous snow-falls, and the white icy night meshed neatly with my personal storms.

When we reached a place in the streets where a wide swath had been plowed. Nancy slowed, turned toward me, and said: 'Okay. What was Tres Toros?'

I remained silent for some time, then reminded her of the family rule we had agreed upon at marriage: 'The house is your domain. The Army is mine.' But then, like a clever lawyer, she cited the elaboration which she had insisted on: 'I can ask two questions in the area of the subject, and you must answer them unless they touch too close to secret matters. Do you agree that I'm entitled to my two questions?'

'I do.'

'Were you authorized to do whatever you did?'

'I play by the book. You know that.' But after reflection, I added: 'Zack thinks I'm in trouble mainly because those who gave the authorization have already publicly denied it.'

'Was money involved?'

'A great deal. But I don't have to tell you that none stuck to my fingers.'

'Did the money come from the Iran caper?'

This question I was not allowed to answer, so I merely said: 'That's three strikes, and you're out.'

Suddenly she pulled the car over to the side of a snowbank, stopped it, turned toward me, and flung her arms about my neck. After kissing me, she whispered: 'Oh, Norman, I love you so much. You've always been so damned decent.' We sat there for some minutes, each aware of how tremendously important the other was, and my storm subsided.

Our gesture of mutual reassurance was rudely broken by two burly men who flashed bright lights into our car and growled: 'What's going on in there?' They were police, and to them we were suspicious prowlers in a residential district.

On the spur of the moment I said: 'My wife felt a little faint,' and after inspecting us closely, the older cop asked: 'Well, if she's dizzy, shouldn't you be driving?' and I had to agree, so I got out in the snow, walked around the car, and started to get in the driver's side while she scrunched over to mine without leaving the car.

'I'm sure you have a driver's license,' the lead cop said. 'And your registration.' Couples our age stopped in a snowbank at dusk aren't too common, so I brought out my license, and when they saw my address they whistled.

'You a professor or something?'

'Army major.' The younger cop saluted and said: 'Sorry to have caused you any inconvenience,' and off they went.

When we reached my parents' snug house and felt the warmth of both the place and the occupants, we relaxed, and since the Sunday papers had been full of the fact that I was to testify tomorrow, Mom and Dad had to be aware of my tension, but they were almost amusingly casual, careful to avoid any mention of Iran, the contras, or the man they knew to be my associate, Oliver North.

As they moved about setting the table while I read the sports pages, I thought how truly American they were and how close they stood to the heart of our mainstream. My father was a certified military hero with a wooden leg to prove it, and my mother . . . that quiet, powerful lady was a civilian heroine laden with her own kind of honors.

Born on the edge of Philadelphia to a family of little means, Rachael Denham went to a public school, where her marks were so striking that she won a scholarship to Bryn Mawr, but because she could not afford a college dormitory or buy even a used car, she had to commute each day on the Pennsylvania Railroad, walking six blocks to the station and a long distance from the Bryn Mawr platform to the college. The travel must have done her good, because she earned phenomenal grades and a better scholarship each year.

As a military man I didn't like Bryn Mawr very much because it was one of those Quaker schools which preach pacifism, and that never gets a nation very far. But it is also a college which requires students to write term papers, and I don't see how anyone can get a serious education without doing that. Anyway, in the winter term of her junior year, in 1948, a serious professor—as you can see, I like that word *serious*—gave her a political-science assignment that baffled her: 'In the decades ahead, malapportionment is bound to be a red-hot political issue. Find out the facts about Pennsylvania.' That was all. He'd never discussed apportionment of any kind in class, so she was on her own.

Well, I've seen her paper. It could have been published, because in her dogged way she reported not only on Pennsylvania but on nine other states, too, revealing just what her professor hoped she would: that across America people who lived in cities and large towns were grotesquely discriminated against in favor of people who lived in small towns or on farms. As the professor had known when he assigned the paper, her home state of Pennsylvania was among the worst. It had sixty-seven counties, many of them wooded rural areas with few people, many more deer, and of great value only in the four weeks of hunting season. It also had two big cities, Philadelphia and Pittsburgh, with large populations. But because there was a tradition that each county must have its own representation in the lower house, ridiculous imbalances occurred which the rural legislators would not allow to be corrected. When my mother saw the raw data, she cried: 'Find me an adding machine!' and with it she produced a series of charts whose squiggly lines portrayed an ugly situation:

For example, here is Forest County with 4,944 and it has its representative, and here's the city of Chester with 66,039, but it also gets one seat.

So a farmer voting in Forest has 13.36 times as much civic power as the city clerk in Chester. I think conservative Pennsylvania, afraid of what it calls 'the corruption of big cities,' wants to keep it that way.

Her charts demonstrated that in the state Senate, which exercised great power, the situation was equally unfair:

I show you three small counties with a combined population of 101,210, and they have one senator, but here is an urban area with 441,518 people, and it has one senator too, which means that the farmer is four times as important as the city man.

Mother prepared figures showing how an absurdly small minority in the rural community could determine what happened in the legislature. She concluded by pointing out:

And because Pennsylvania sends congressmen to Washington in accordance with local districting, our federal legislature is also grossly affected by the overrepresentation of rural areas and underrepresentation of cities. This imbalance results in national legislation that is sometimes absurd.

I'm told that many young people have the course of their lives determined by the term papers they write in college, and that was certainly the case with my mother. The facts she uncovered in researching this one paper so captivated her that she spent what should have been her senior year as an aide to a Pennsylvania senator in Washington. In her next year back at Bryn Mawr, she organized a conference attended by students from all parts of the nation: 'Malapportionment in State Legislatures,' and her opening speech to the delegates dealt with 'The Refusal of the Tennessee Legislature to Reapportion.'

My wife and I have a copy:

> The Tennessee constitution requires a fresh reapportionment of districts following each decennial census, but rural legislators, who vastly outnumber urban, refuse to make any changes which might diminish their numbers. The result? Since 1901 there has been no reapportionment in Tennessee, and the cities suffer. Is there any force within the state capable of making the state conform to its own law? None.

It was the long discussion conducted at that convention which convinced my mother, and many bright young people like her, that the only agency powerful enough to make the states obey their own laws—and there were half a dozen as badly out of balance as Tennessee—was the United States Supreme Court.

'Because,' she pointed out, with an astuteness far beyond her years, 'the federal Congress is itself voted into power by districts which are also just as badly unbalanced.'

'Not senators,' a young man from Alabama corrected. 'They're elected statewide,' and she replied: 'You're right. But most of them get to be senators by being congressmen first. They band together to protect the bad old system which produced them.'

By accident my mother had stumbled upon her life's work. Before she left Bryn Mawr she was an expert in apportionment, and by the time she got her Ph.D. from Smith, she was being invited to address various state legislatures and counsel on problems facing them when new census figures came in. Her numerous publications on the subject attracted such favorable attention that she was offered positions at various universities, including Chicago, but because she wanted to be near Congress, she chose Georgetown, which made it easy for her to heckle the government in its shameful failure to do what clearly had to be done. In an article published in 1960 she wrote:

> I am totally frustrated. Every concerned man and woman in the United States knows what ought to be done to assure justice to the people of the cities, but there is no way to force action. What in common sense can we do? Congress will never take steps to launch a constitutional

amendment. State legislatures refuse to cleanse themselves. You and I are powerless to do anything. Where can a citizen look for help?

But she did not allow her obsession to become a monomania: 'Always I kept before me the example of Emily Starr, who sacrificed her personal happiness on the altar of political reform, and I wanted none of that. I kept my voice down when consulting with legislators. I wore good-looking clothes and was deferential to elderly men who had spent their lives in government. But when the going got tough . . . boy, did I stick it to them!'

One of the most vivid memories of my life is sitting with her and my two sisters and hearing her tell how she met our father, 'the war hero' as she always referred to him when teasing: 'I was an underpaid, undernourished beginning professor at Bryn Mawr, just getting my feet wet in the academic world. And to tell you the truth, I was a wee bit desperate about finding a husband. Then your father appeared on campus to speak at an assembly of some kind. Marvelous uniform, medals on his chest, wooden leg adding mystery. Oh, did I ever fall in love.'

'Did his leg sort of off-steer you?' my sister once asked, and Mother gave a remarkably frank answer: 'Some women in the faculty club asked that, and I told them: "So far as I know, the left leg has nothing to do with love or the production of fertile sperm," and you adorable kids are the proof of that.'

Then came the exciting news. The Supreme Court

agreed to hear arguments regarding the failure of state legislatures to reapportion, and what state do you suppose they chose as the prime example? The very one my mother had identified years before: Tennessee! The case was called *Baker* v. *Carr*, and Mother was invited to testify as an amicus curiae, informed friend of the court, or as she told us: 'In my case an amica curiae, since I am a woman.'

We have copies of her argument:

> When the American people can find redress in no other agency of government, none, and we have exhausted them all, we must throw ourselves on the mercy of this Court, which was established to provide remedy in just such impasses. You are our defense against frustration and despair. Only your Court can order justice to be done.

On 26 March 1962, when I was eleven years old, Mother sat with us at home listening to the radio as the news came that the Supreme Court had agreed with her, 6 to 2, meaning that at long last, the states would be forced to break the logjam which had imprisoned the cities. She did not exult. She listened to several different stations giving guesses as to what *Baker* v. *Carr* meant, then she prepared supper.

That night fellow professors and newspaper people trooped in to congratulate her, and she told them:

'The tools are always there to mend our democracy. Problem is, find someone to use them.'

'Won't you be pretty busy now, advising the various legislatures?' a reporter asked, and she said: 'That's what I've been doing for the past dozen years, and frankly, I didn't accomplish much. The decision promises nothing. It's how we use it that counts.'

After supper we sat for a while, talking about everything but what I would be doing the next day. When Nancy and I left, Mother walked with us to our car, and said quietly: 'Norm, your father and I were tremendously proud when you were invited to work in the White House. We hope we can be just as proud of the manner in which you leave.'

Norman
Starr

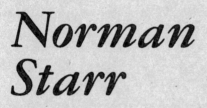

1951–

ON MONDAY, Nancy rose early, laid out my uniform, and attached the neat rows of colorful ribbons which attested to my years in service. The American military hands out decorations the way a Sunday School gives awards for attendance, but they do impress civilians, and that was the purpose today. But if I did wear some medals for actions of only routine consequence, I had no medal testifying to the considerable contributions I had made to the security of our nation in Central America. You win some, you lose some.

While I was shaving, Nancy sprang a surprise which I did not appreciate. She called into the bathroom: 'I asked Dad to stop by for breakfast,' and I was about to groan 'Not today,' when I restrained myself, because Professor Makinowsky was a major reason why his daughter was such an admirable wife and citizen.

I had courted Nancy Makin for nearly two disorganized years before I learned that she had shortened her name, but as we became more serious, she said one day: 'I want you to meet my father. He's something, professor of history in a jerkwater two-year college, and a great man. Name's Makinowsky from a corner where Poland and Czechoslovakia touched.'

When he appeared that day, he was a professor out of Central Casting: short like Nancy, big head of unruly black hair, inquisitive like her, and a joy to talk with. His degrees were a mixed bag, one from Prague, two from those big, grubby institutions in New York City that don't play football, so he never progressed beyond the little school in Maryland, where he became the most popular teacher on campus.

Now, when he looked at me standing there in my uniform with its rows of bright ribbons, he broke into laughter: 'When we landed in England on our way to Normandy in World War II with our medals glaring, a British Tommy shouted: "Blimey! Their whole bloody army is heroes!" '

Nancy interrupted, because like always, she was

determined to talk sense: 'I wanted Father to tell you a story, Norman. One that's influenced me profoundly.' Nancy uses the word *profound* a good deal, because she likes to allocate her time to profound subjects.

Makinowsky, holding his coffee cup in both hands, peered over the rim, pondering how to start. Then, coughing deferentially, he said: 'One of the most reassuring court decisions of my lifetime has attracted little attention. But I stress it with my students. The facts were straightforward. A married couple in a Western state, I think it might have been Utah. They weren't nice people, really, ran a house of prostitution, using three older women whom they treated abominably. Then one Fourth of July they suddenly decided to give the "girls" a vacation, all expenses paid. Drove them to Yellowstone Park, treated them to a great time, and as they drove home to put the girls back to work, they said "Girls, we appreciate your help," and the girls said "Thanks."

'Well, the Utah authorities arrested the couple for violating the Mann Act, bringing the women back across the Utah state line for immoral purposes. Caught dead to rights, no contest, big fine and long prison sentences for the culprits.'

'What's the point?' I asked, my irritation showing at such a rambling interruption on a day of some importance to me.

'Like I said, it went to the state court, and some judge wrote a most moving decision. Said the facts in the case were irrefutable, the Mann Act had been transgressed, a crime had been committed, and the punishment was not unreasonable. But, he added, sometimes the law hands down a judgment which offends the rule of common sense. This was an example. The state of Utah could properly have arrested this couple at any time during the past dozen years for wrongs that they were committing, but they waited until the pair was doing the right thing . . . bringing their girls back from a paid holiday. The sense of propriety on which society must rely had been offended. Case reversed. Couple set free.'

My father-in-law's narration hit me like a round of mortar fire. *The sense of propriety had been offended.* I looked at this grizzled fighter, survivor of the dreadful wars of Central Europe, patient teacher of young Americans who were striving to formulate their own judgments of right and wrong, and I suddenly understood what he was saying: 'You think that for United States military officers to stand before the public in full uniform and take the Fifth Amendment offends the rule of common sense?'

'Norman, you have every right to take the Fifth. Tens of millions of people in Europe and around the world wish their governments gave them such a right. No more tortures, no more of what the Soviets did to my brother to make him incriminate himself.'

'But for military officers whose job it is . . .' My voice trailed off.

'Yes, it is offensive. Your job is to protect the nation, not yourself.'

It must have been apparent to Nancy and her father that I was frightened of what might happen to my wife if I went to prison, for they both started to offer solutions at once. Nancy prevailed: 'I told you I can still handle data processing. I can sweat it out,' and her father said: "I have savings.'

I dropped my head and mumbled: 'Takes a refugee from God-knows-where to teach me my own law.'

Makinowsky said reassuringly: 'Norman, in the Watergate crisis it required an Italian judge, Sirica, a Polish lawyer, Jaworski, and a black congress-woman from Texas, Jordan, whose grandfather had probably been a slave, to sort things out. And maybe save our Union. You don't always have to find a white Anglo-Saxon Protestant whose ancestors served in the Revolution to do the job. Maybe it takes some simple peasant from Czechoslovakia to point out the truth.' His voice became sharp, and with his daughter beside him, he repeated: 'Some things are offensive to the rule of common sense. And what you're about to do is one of them.'

At this moment Zack McMaster came into the kitchen, saw me in my uniform, ribbons in order, and said: 'Good, I see you're ready.'

I was indeed, but not for what Zack wanted me to do, and as I looked at him in his proper three-piece suit, I was struck by one of those blinding flashes which can sometimes illuminate a human life, or, I think, the life of a nation. I knew that I would not face the Senate Committee alone. With me would be: Old Jared Starr defiantly signing a declaration which might have caused him to be hanged. Simon

Starr, silent in the great debate, powerful in the nighttime argument. Fat old Edmund Starr, sometimes not sure of the legal facts but always determined to uphold what John Marshall assured him was the reasonable decision. Hugh Starr, faithfully supporting Robert E. Lee in a forlorn cause. And courageous Emily Starr, standing alone, against scorn and humiliation and abandonment, to do a job which had to be done.

They were my peers, my counselors, they and my wife and my good father-in-law, and I had come perilously close to ignoring them. I now saw the Constitution which my ancestors had helped create, interpret and enlarge as a treasured legacy whose provisions bind the various regions and interests of our nation together. Philosophically as evanescent as a whispering wind, structurally more powerful than steel cables, that superb document will be effective only if each new generation believes in it—and keeps it renewed.

Slipping out of my military blouse and into an ordinary suit jacket that more or less went with my trousers, I told a startled McMaster: 'I'm ready,' and off we marched to the Senate.

The Constitution of the United States

WE THE PEOPLE of the United States, in order to form a more perfect union, establish justice, insure domestic tranquility, provide for the common defense, promote the general welfare, and secure the blessings of liberty to ourselves and our posterity, do ordain and establish this Constitution for the United States of America.

Article I

SECTION 1   All legislative powers herein granted shall be vested in a Congress of the United States, which shall consist of a Senate and House of Representatives.

SECTION 2   (1) The House of Representatives shall be composed of members chosen every second year by the people of the several States, and the electors in each State shall have the qualifications requisite for electors of the most numerous branch of the State legislature.

(2) No person shall be a Representative who shall not have attained to the age of twenty-five years, and been seven years a citizen of the United States and who shall not, when elected, be an inhabitant of that State in which he shall be chosen.

(3) Representatives and direct taxes shall be appor-

tioned among the several States which may be included within this Union, according to their respective numbers, which shall be determined by adding to the whole number of free persons, including those bound to service for a term of years, and excluding Indians not taxed, three fifths of all other persons. The actual enumeration shall be made within three years after the first meeting of the Congress of the United States, and within every subsequent term of ten years, in such manner as they shall by law direct. The number of Representatives shall not exceed one for every thirty thousand, but each State shall have at least one Representative; and until such enumeration shall be made, the State of New Hampshire shall be entitled to choose three, Massachusetts eight, Rhode Island and Providence Plantations one, Connecticut five, New York six, New Jersey four, Pennsylvania eight, Delaware one, Maryland six, Virginia ten, North Carolina five, South Carolina five, and Georgia three.

(4) When vacancies happen in the representation from any State, the executive authority thereof shall issue writs of election to fill such vacancies.

(5) The House of Representatives shall choose their Speaker and other officers; and shall have the sole power of impeachment.

SECTION 3   (1) The Senate of the United States shall be composed of two Senators from each State, chosen by the legislature thereof, for six years; and each Senator shall have one vote.

(2) Immediately after they shall be assembled in consequence of the first election, they shall be divided as equally as may be into three classes. The seats of the Senators of the first class shall be vacated at the expiration of the second year, of the second class at the expiration of the fourth year, and of the third class at the expiration of the sixth year, so that one third may be chosen every second year; and if vacancies happen

by resignation, or otherwise, during the recess of the legislature of any State, the executive thereof may make temporary appointments until the next meeting of the legislature, which shall then fill such vacancies.

(3) No person shall be a Senator who shall not have attained to the age of thirty years, and been nine years a citizen of the United States, and who shall not, when elected, be an inhabitant of that State for which he shall be chosen.

(4) The Vice President of the United States shall be president of the Senate, but shall have no vote, unless they be equally divided.

(5) The Senate shall choose their other officers, and also a president pro tempore, in the absence of the Vice President, or when he shall exercise the office of President of the United States.

(6) The Senate shall have the sole power to try all impeachments. When sitting for that purpose, they shall be on oath or affirmation. When the President of the United States is tried, the Chief Justice shall preside: and no person shall be convicted without the concurrence of two thirds of the members present.

(7) Judgment in cases of impeachment shall not extend further than to removal from office, and disqualification to hold and enjoy any office of honor, trust or profit under the United States: but the party convicted shall nevertheless be liable and subject to indictment, trial, judgment and punishment, according to law.

SECTION 4   (1) The times, places and manner of holding elections for Senators and Representatives, shall be prescribed in each State by the legislature thereof; but the Congress may at any time by law make or alter such regulations, except as to the places of choosing Senators.

(2) The Congress shall assemble at least once in every year, and such meeting shall be on the first Monday in

December, unless they shall by law appoint a different day.

SECTION 5 (1) Each House shall be the judge of the elections, returns and qualifications of its own members, and a majority of each shall constitute a quorum to do business; but a smaller number may adjourn from day to day, and may be authorized to compel the attendance of absent members, in such manner, and under such penalties as each House may provide.

(2) Each House may determine the rules of its proceedings, punish its members for disorderly behavior, and, with the concurrence of two thirds, expel a member.

(3) Each House shall keep a journal of its proceedings, and from time to time publish the same, excepting such parts as may in their judgment require secrecy; and the yeas and nays of the members of either House on any question shall, at the desire of one fifth of those present, be entered on the journal.

(4) Neither House, during the session of Congress, shall, without the consent of the other, adjourn for more than three days, nor to any other place than that in which the two Houses shall be sitting.

SECTION 6 (1) The Senators and Representatives shall receive a compensation for their services, to be ascertained by law, and paid out of the Treasury of the United States. They shall in all cases, except treason, felony and breach of the peace, be privileged from arrest during their attendance at the session of their respective Houses, and in going to and returning from the same; and for any speech or debate in either House, they shall not be questioned in any other place.

(2) No Senator or Representative shall, during the time for which he was elected, be appointed to any civil office under the authority of the United States, which shall have been created, or the emoluments whereof

shall have been increased during such time; and no person holding any office under the United States, shall be a member of either House during his continuance in office.

SECTION 7   (1) All bills for raising revenue shall originate in the House of Representatives; but the Senate may propose or concur with amendments as on other bills.

(2) Every bill which shall have passed the House of Representatives and the Senate shall, before it become a law, be presented to the President of the United States; if he approve he shall sign it, but if not he shall return it, with his objections to that House in which it shall have originated, who shall enter the objections at large on their journal, and proceed to reconsider it. If after such reconsideration two thirds of that House shall agree to pass the bill, it shall be sent, together with the objections, to the other House, by which it shall likewise be reconsidered, and if approved by two thirds of that House, it shall become a law. But in all such cases the votes of both Houses shall be determined by yeas and nays, and the names of the persons voting for and against the bill shall be entered on the journal of each House respectively. If any bill shall not be returned by the President within ten days (Sundays excepted) after it shall have been presented to him, the same shall be a law, in like manner as if he had signed it, unless the Congress by their adjournment prevent its return, in which case it shall not be a law.

(3) Every order, resolution, or vote to which the concurrence of the Senate and House of Representatives may be necessary (except on a question of adjournment) shall be presented to the President of the United States; and before the same shall take effect, shall be approved by him, or being disapproved by him, shall be repassed by two thirds of the Senate and House of

Representatives, according to the rules and limitations prescribed in the case of a bill.

SECTION 8 (1) The Congress shall have power to lay and collect taxes, duties, imposts and excises, to pay the debts and provide for the common defense and general welfare of the United States; but all duties, imposts and excises shall be uniform throughout the United States;

(2) To borrow money on the credit of the United States;

(3) To regulate commerce with foreign nations, and among the several States, and with the Indian tribes;

(4) To establish a uniform rule of naturalization, and uniform laws on the subject of bankruptcies throughout the United States;

(5) To coin money, regulate the value thereof, and of foreign coin, and fix the standard of weights and measures;

(6) To provide for the punishment of counterfeiting the securities and current coin of the United States;

(7) To establish post offices and post roads;

(8) To promote the progress of science and useful arts, by securing for limited times to authors and inventors the exclusive right to their respective writings and discoveries;

(9) To constitute tribunals inferior to the Supreme Court;

(10) To define and punish piracies and felonies committed on the high seas, and offenses against the law of nations;

(11) To declare war, grant letters of marque and reprisal, and make rules concerning captures on land and water;

(12) To raise and support armies, but no appropriation of money to that use shall be for a longer term than two years;

(13) To provide and maintain a navy;

(14) To make rules for the government and regulation of the land and naval forces;

(15) To provide for calling forth the militia to execute the laws of the Union, suppress insurrections and repel invasions;

(16) To provide for organizing, arming, and disciplining the militia, and for governing such part of them as may be employed in the service of the United States, reserving to the States respectively, the appointment of the officers, and the authority of training the militia according to the discipline prescribed by Congress;

(17) To exercise exclusive legislation in all cases whatsoever, over such district (not exceeding ten miles square) as may, by cession of particular States, and the acceptance of Congress, become the seat of the government of the United States, and to exercise like authority over all places purchased by the consent of the legislature of the State in which the same shall be, for the erection of forts, magazines, dockyards, and other needful buildings; and

(18) To make all laws which shall be necessary and proper for carrying into execution the foregoing powers, and all other powers vested by this Constitution in the government of the United States, or in any department or officer thereof.

SECTION 9 (1) The migration or importation of such persons as any of the States now existing shall think proper to admit, shall not be prohibited by the Congress prior to the year one thousand eight hundred and eight, but a tax or duty may be imposed on such importation, not exceeding ten dollars for each person.

(2) The privilege of the *writ of habeas corpus* shall not be suspended, unless when in cases of rebellion or invasion the public safety may require it.

(3) No bill of attainder or ex post facto law shall be passed.

(4) No capitation, or other direct, tax shall be laid,

unless in proportion to the census or enumeration herein before directed to be taken.

(5) No tax or duty shall be laid on articles exported from any State.

(6) No preference shall be given by any regulation of commerce or revenue to the ports of one State over those of another: nor shall vessels bound to, or from, one State, be obliged to enter, clear, or pay duties in another.

(7) No money shall be drawn from the Treasury, but in consequence of appropriations made by law; and a regular statement and account of the receipts and expenditures of all public money shall be published from time to time.

(8) No title of nobility shall be granted by the United States: and no person holding any office of profit or trust under them, shall, without the consent of the Congress, accept of any present, emolument, office, or title, of any kind whatever, from any king, prince, or foreign State.

Section 10   (1) No State shall enter into any treaty, alliance, or confederation; grant letters of marque and reprisal; coin money; emit bills of credit; make anything but gold and silver coin a tender in payment of debts; pass any bill of attainder, ex post facto law, or law impairing the obligation of contracts, or grant any title of nobility.

(2) No State shall, without the consent of Congress, lay any imposts or duties on imports or exports, except what may be absolutely necessary for executing its inspection laws; and the net produce of all duties and imposts, laid by any State on imports or exports, shall be for the use of the Treasury of the United States; and all such laws shall be subject to the revision and control of the Congress.

(3) No State shall, without the consent of Congress, lay any duty of tonnage, keep troops, or ships of war

in time of peace, enter into any agreement or compact with another State, or with a foreign power, or engage in war, unless actually invaded, or in such imminent danger as will not admit of delay.

Article II

SECTION 1 (1) The executive power shall be vested in a President of the United States of America. He shall hold his office during the term of four years, and, together with the Vice President, chosen for the same term, be elected, as follows:

(2) Each State shall appoint, in such manner as the legislature thereof may direct, a number of electors, equal to the whole number of Senators and Representatives to which the State may be entitled in the Congress: but no Senator or Representative, or person holding an office of trust or profit under the United States, shall be appointed an elector.

The electors shall meet in their respective States, and vote by ballot for two persons, of whom one at least shall not be an inhabitant of the same State with themselves. And they shall make a list of all the persons voted for, and of the number of votes for each; which list they shall sign and certify, and transmit sealed to the seat of the government of the United States, directed to the president of the Senate. The president of the Senate shall, in the presence of the Senate and House of Representatives, open all the certificates, and the votes shall then be counted. The person having the greatest number of votes shall be the President, if such number be a majority of the whole number of electors appointed; and if there be more than one who have such majority, and have an equal number of votes, then the House of Representatives shall immediately choose by ballot one of them for President; and if no person have a majority, then from the five highest on the list the said House shall in like manner choose the President. But in choosing the President, the votes shall be taken by States, the representation from each State having one vote; a quorum for this purpose shall consist of a member or members from two thirds of the States, and a majority of all the States shall be necessary to a choice. In every case, after the choice of the President, the person having the greatest number of votes of the electors shall be the Vice President. But if there should remain two or more who have equal votes, the Senate shall choose from them by ballot the Vice President.

(3) The Congress may determine the time of choosing the electors, and the day on which they shall give their votes; which day shall be the same throughout the United States.

(4) No person except a natural born citizen, or a citizen of the United States, at the time of the adoption of this Constitution, shall be eligible to the office of President; neither shall any person be eligible to that office who shall not have attained to the age of thirty five years, and been fourteen years a resident within the United States.

(5) In the case of the removal of the President from office, or of his death, resignation, or inability to discharge the powers and duties of the said office, the same shall devolve on the Vice President, and the Congress may by law provide for the case of removal, death, resignation, or inability, both of the President and Vice President, declaring what officer shall then act as president, and such officer shall act accordingly, until the disability be removed, or a President shall be elected.

(6) The President shall, at stated times, receive for his services, a compensation, which shall neither be increased nor diminished during the period for which he shall have been elected, and he shall not receive

within that period any other emolument from the United States, or any of them.

(7) Before he enter on the execution of his office, he shall take the following oath or affirmation:—"I do solemnly swear (or affirm) that I will faithfully execute the office of the President of the United States, and will to the best of my ability, preserve, protect and defend the Constitution of the United States."

SECTION 2   (1) The President shall be commander in chief of the army and navy of the United States, and of the militia of the several States, when called into the actual service of the United States; he may require the opinion, in writing, of the principal officer in each of the executive departments, upon any subject relating to the duties of their respective offices, and he shall have power to grant reprieves and pardons for offenses against the United States, except in cases of impeachment.

(2) He shall have power, by and with the advice and consent of the Senate, to make treaties, provided two thirds of the Senators present concur; and he shall nominate, and by and with the advice and consent of the Senate, shall appoint ambassadors, other public ministers and consuls, judges of the Supreme Court, and all other officers of the United States, whose appointments are not herein otherwise provided for, and which shall be established by law: but the Congress may by law vest the appointment of such inferior officers, as they think proper, in the President alone, in the courts of law, or in the heads of departments.

(3) The President shall have power to fill up all vacancies that may happen during the recess of the Senate, by granting commissions which shall expire at the end of their next session.

SECTION 3   He shall from time to time give to the Congress information of the state of the Union, and recommend to their consideration such measures as he shall judge necessary and expedient; he may, on extraordinary occasions, convene both Houses, or either of them, and in case of disagreement between them, with respect to the time of adjournment, he may adjourn them to such time as he shall think proper; he shall receive ambassadors and other public ministers; he shall take that the laws be faithfully executed, and shall commission all the officers of the United States.

SECTION 4 The President, Vice President and all civil officers of the United States, shall be removed from office on impeachment for, and conviction of, treason, bribery, or other high crimes and misdemeanors.

Article III

SECTION 1 The judicial power of the United States shall be vested in one Supreme Court, and in such inferior courts as the Congress may from time to time ordain and establish. The judges, both of the Supreme and inferior courts, shall hold their offices during good behavior, and shall, at stated times, receive for their services, a compensation, which shall not be diminished during their continuance in office.

SECTION 2 (1) The judicial power shall extend to all cases, in law and equity, arising under this Constitution, the laws of the United States, and treaties made, or which shall be made, under their authority;—to all cases affecting ambassadors, other public ministers and consuls;—to all cases of admiralty and maritime jurisdiction;—to controversies to which the United States shall be a party;—to controversies between two or more States;—between a State and citizens of another State;—between citizens of different States;—between citizens of the same State claiming lands under grants of different States, and between a State, or the citizens thereof, and foreign States, citizens or subjects.

(2) In all cases affecting ambassadors, other public ministers and consuls, and those in which a State shall be party, the Supreme Court shall have original jurisdiction. In all the other cases before mentioned, the Supreme Court shall have appellate jurisdiction, both

as to law and fact, with such exceptions, and under such regulations as the Congress shall make.

(3) The trial of all crimes, except in cases of impeachment, shall be by jury; and such trial shall be held in the State where the said crimes shall have been committed; but when not committed within any State, the trial shall be at such place or places as the Congress may by law have directed.

SECTION 3   (1) Treason against the United States, shall consist only in levying war against them, or in adhering to their enemies, giving them aid and comfort. No person shall be convicted of treason unless on the testimony of two witnesses to the same overt act, or on confession in open court.

(2) The Congress shall have power to declare the punishment of treason, but no attainder of treason shall work corruption of blood, or forfeiture except during the life of the person attainted.

Article IV

SECTION 1 Full faith and credit shall be given in each State to the public acts, records, and judicial proceedings of every other State. And the Congress may by general laws prescribe the manner in which such acts, records and proceedings shall be proved, and the effect thereof.

SECTION 2 (1) The citizens of each State shall be entitled to all privileges and immunities of citizens in the several States.

(2) A person charged in any State with treason, felony, or other crime, who shall flee from justice, and be found in another State, shall on demand of the executive authority of the State from which he fled, be delivered up, to be removed to the State having jurisdiction of the crime.

(3) No person held to service or labor in one State, under the laws thereof, escaping into another, shall, in consequence of any law or regulation therein, be discharged from such service or labor, but shall be delivered up on claim of the party to whom such service or labor may be due.

SECTION 3 (1) New States may be admitted by the Congress into this Union; but no new State shall be formed or erected within the jurisdiction of any other State; nor any State be formed by the junction of two or more States, or parts of States, without the consent of the legislatures of the States concerned as well as of the Congress.

(2) The Congress shall have power to dispose of and make all needful rules and regulations respecting the territory or other property belonging to the United States; and nothing in this Constitution shall be so construed as to prejudice any claims of the United States, or of any particular State.

SECTION 4 The United States shall guarantee to every State in this Union a republican form of government, and shall protect each of them against invasion; and on application of the legislature, or of the executive (when the legislature cannot be convened) against domestic violence.

Article V

The Congress, whenever two thirds of both Houses shall deem it necessary, shall propose amendments to this Constitution, or, on the application of the legislatures of two thirds of the several States, shall call a convention for proposing amendments, which, in either case, shall be valid to all intents and purposes, as part of this Constitution, when ratified by the legislatures of three fourths of the several States, or by conventions in three fourths thereof, as the one or the other mode of ratification may be proposed by the Congress; Provided that no amendment which may be made prior to the year one thousand eight hundred and eight shall in any manner affect the first and fourth clauses in the ninth section of the first article; and that no State, without its consent, shall be deprived of its equal suffrage in the Senate.

Article VI

SECTION 1   All debts contracted and engagements entered into, before the adoption of this Constitution, shall be as valid against the United States under this Constitution, as under the Confederation.

SECTION 2   This Constitution, and the laws of the United States which shall be made in pursuance thereof; and all treaties made, or which shall be made, under the authority of the United States, shall be the supreme law of the land; and the judges in every State shall be bound thereby, anything in the constitution or laws of any State to the contrary notwithstanding.

SECTION 3   The Senators and Representatives before mentioned, and the members of the several State legislatures, and all executive and judicial officers, both of the United States and of the several States, shall be bound by oath or affirmation to support this Constitution; but no religious test shall ever be required as a qualification to anv office or public trust under the United States.

Article VII

The ratification of the conventions of nine States, shall be sufficient for the establishment of this Constitution between the States so ratifying the same.
DONE in Convention by the unanimous consent of the States present the seventeenth day of September in the year of our Lord one thousand seven hundred and eighty-seven, and of the independence of the United States of America the twelfth.

In Witness whereof We have hereunto subscribed our Names.

GEORGE WASHINGTON
President and deputy from Virginia

New Hampshire.
JOHN LANGDON
NICHOLAS GILMAN

Massachusetts.
NATHANIEL GORHAM
RUFUS KING

New Jersey.
WILLIAM LIVINGSTON
DAVID BREARLEY
WILLIAM PATERSON
JONATHAN DAYTON

Pennsylvania.
BENJAMIN FRANKLIN
ROBERT MORRIS
THOMAS FITZSIMONS
JAMES WILSON
THOMAS MIFFLIN
GEORGE CLYMER
JARED INGERSOLL
GOUVERNEUR MORRIS

Delaware.
GEORGE READ
JOHN DICKINSON
JACOB BROOM
GUNNING BEDFORD, JR.
RICHARD BASSETT

Georgia.
WILLIAM FEW
ABRAHAM BALDWIN

Connecticut.
WILLIAM SAMUEL JOHNSON
ROGER SHERMAN

New York.
ALEXANDER HAMILTON

Maryland.
JAMES MCHENRY
DANIEL CARROL
DANIEL OF ST. THOMAS
JENIFER

Virginia.
JOHN BLAIR
JAMES MADISON JR.

North Carolina.
WILLIAM BLOUNT
HUGH WILLIAMSON
RICHARD DOBBS SPAIGHT

South Carolina.
JOHN RUTLEDGE
CHARLES PINCKNEY
CHARLES COTESWORTH
PINCKNEY
PIERCE BUTLER

Attest:
WILLIAM JACKSON, *Secretary*

ARTICLES in addition to and AMENDMENTS of the Constitution of the United States of America, proposed by Congress, and ratified by the legislatures of the several States, pursuant to the fifth article of the original Constitution.

Article I*

Congress shall make no law respecting an establishment of religion, or prohibiting the free exercise thereof; or abridging the freedom of speech, or of the press; or the right of the people peaceably to assemble, and to petition the government for a redress of grievances.

Article II

A well regulated militia, being necessary to the security of a free State, the right of the people to keep and bear arms, shall not be infringed.

Article III

No soldier shall, in time of peace be quartered in any house, without the consent of the owner, nor in time of war, but in a manner to be prescribed by law.

* The first ten Amendments were adopted in 1791.

Article IV

The right of the people to be secure in their persons, houses, papers, and effects, against unreasonable searches and seizures, shall not be violated, and no warrants shall issue, but upon probable cause, supported by oath or affirmation, and particularly describing the place to be searched, and the persons or things to be seized.

Article V

No person shall be held to answer for a capital, or otherwise infamous crime, unless on a presentment or indictment of a grand jury, except in cases arising in the land or naval forces, or in the militia, when in actual service in time of war or public danger; nor shall any person be subject for the same offense to be twice put in jeopardy of life or limb; nor shall be compelled in any criminal case to be a witness against himself, nor be deprived of life, liberty, or property, without due process of law; nor shall private property be taken for public use, without just compensation.

Article VI

In all criminal prosecutions the accused shall enjoy the right to a speedy and public trial, by an impartial jury of the State and district wherein the crime shall have been committed, which district shall have been previously ascertained by law, and to be informed of the nature and cause of the accusation; to be confronted with the witnesses against him; to have compulsory process for obtaining witnesses in his favor, and to have the assistance of counsel for his defense.

Article VII

In suits at common law, where the value in controversy shall exceed twenty dollars, the right of trial by jury shall be preserved, and no fact tried by a jury shall be otherwise reexamined in any court of the United States, than according to the rules of the common law.

Article VIII

Excessive bail shall not be required, nor excessive fines imposed, nor cruel and unusual punishments inflicted.

Article IX

The enumeration in the Constitution, of certain rights, shall not be construed to deny or disparage others retained by the people.

Article X

The powers not delegated to the United States by the Constitution, nor prohibited by it to the States, are reserved to the States respectively, or to the people.

Article XI*

The judicial power of the United States shall not be construed to extend to any suit in law or equity, commenced or prosecuted against one of the United States

* Ratified in 1795; proclaimed in 1798.

by citizens of another State, or by citizens or subjects of any foreign State.

Article XII*

The electors shall meet in their respective States and vote by ballot for President and Vice-President, one of whom, at least, shall not be an inhabitant of the same State with themselves; they shall name in their ballots the person voted for as President, and in distinct ballots the person voted for as Vice-President, and they shall make distinct lists of all persons voted for as President, and of all persons voted for as Vice-President, and of the number of votes for each, which lists they shall sign and certify, and transmit sealed to the seat of the government of the United States, directed to the president of the Senate;—The president of the Senate shall, in the presence of the Senate and House of Representatives, open all the certificates and the votes shall then be counted;—The person having the greatest number of votes for President, shall be the President, if such number be a majority of the whole number of electors appointed; and if no person have such majority, then from the persons having the highest numbers not exceeding three on the list of those voted for as President, the House of Representatives shall choose immediately, by ballot, the President. But in choosing the President, the votes shall be taken by States, the representation from each State having one vote; a quorum for this purpose shall consist of a member or members from two thirds of the States, and a majority of all the States shall be necessary to a choice. And if the House of Representatives shall not choose a President whenever the right of choice shall devolve upon them, before the fourth day of March next following, then the Vice-

* Adopted in 1804.

President shall act as President, as in the case of the death or other constitutional disability of the President.—The person having the greatest number of votes as Vice-President, shall be the Vice-President, if such number be a majority of the whole number of electors appointed, and if no person have a majority, then from the two highest numbers on the list, the Senate shall choose the Vice-President; a quorum for the purpose shall consist of two thirds of the whole number of Senators, and a majority of the whole number shall be necessary to a choice. But no person constitutionally ineligible to the office of President shall be eligible to that of Vice-President of the United States.

Article XIII*

SECTION 1   Neither slavery nor involuntary servitude, except as a punishment for crime whereof the party shall have been duly convicted, shall exist within the United States, or any place subject to their jurisdiction.

SECTION 2   Congress shall have power to enforce this article by appropriate legislation.

Article XIV†

SECTION 1   All persons born or naturalized in the United States, and subject to the jurisdiction thereof, are citizens of the United States and of the State wherein they reside. No State shall make or enforce any law which shall abridge the privileges or immunities of citizens of the United States; nor shall any State deprive

* Adopted in 1865.
† Adopted in 1868.

any person of life, liberty, or property, without due process of law; nor deny any person within its jurisdiction the equal protection of the laws.

SECTION 2   Representatives shall be apportioned among the several States according to their respective numbers, counting the whole number of persons in each State, excluding Indians not taxed. But when the right to vote at any election for the choice of electors for President and Vice President of the United States, Representatives in Congress, the executive and judicial offices of a State, or the members of the legislature thereof, is denied to any of the male inhabitants of such State, being twenty-one years of age, and citizens of the United States, or in any way abridged, except for participation in rebellion, or other crime, the basis of representation therein shall be reduced in the proportion which the number of such male citizens shall bear to the whole number of male citizens twenty-one years of age in such State.

SECTION 3   No person shall be a Senator or Representative in Congress, or elector of President and Vice President, or hold any office, civil or military, under the United States, or under any State, who, having previously taken an oath, as a member of Congress, or as an officer of the United States, or as a member of any State legislature, or as an executive or judicial officer of any State, to support the Constitution of the United States, shall have engaged in insurrection or rebellion against the same, or given aid or comfort to the enemies thereof. But Congress may by a vote of two thirds of each House, remove such disability.

SECTION 4   The validity of the public debt of the United States, authorized by law, including debts incurred for payment of pensions and bounties for services in suppressing insurrection or rebellion, shall not be questioned. But neither the United States nor any State shall assume or pay any debt or obligation incurred in aid of insurrection or rebellion against the United States, or any claim for the loss or emancipation of any slave; but all such debts, obligations and claims shall be held illegal and void.

SECTION 5   The Congress shall have power to enforce, by appropriate legislation, the provision of this article.

Article XV*

SECTION 1   The right of citizens of the United States to vote shall not be denied or abridged by the United States or by any State on account of race, color, or previous condition of servitude.

SECTION 2   The Congress shall have the power to enforce this article by appropriate legislation.

* Adopted in 1870.

Article XVI*

The Congress shall have the power to lay and collect taxes on incomes, from whatever source derived, without apportionment among the several States, and without regard to any census or enumeration.

Article XVII†

The Senate of the United States shall be composed of two Senators from each State, elected by the people thereof, for six years; and each Senator shall have one vote. The electors in each State shall have the qualifications requisite for electors of the most numerous branch of the State legislatures.

When vacancies happen in the representation of any State in the Senate, the executive authority of such State shall issue writs of election to fill such vacancies: *Provided*, That the legislature of any State may empower the executive thereof to make temporary appointments until the people fill the vacancies by election as the legislature may direct.

This amendment shall not be so construed as to affect the election or term of any Senator chosen before it becomes valid as part of the Constitution.

Article XVIII‡

SECTION 1   After one year from the ratification of this article the manufacture, sale, or transportation of intoxicating liquors within, the importation thereof into, or the exportation thereof from the United States and

---

* Adopted in 1913.
† Adopted in 1913.
‡ Adopted in 1919. Repealed by the 21st Amendment.

all territory subject to the jurisdiction thereof for beverage purposes is hereby prohibited.

SECTION 2 The Congress and the several States shall have concurrent power to enforce this article by appropriate legislation.

SECTION 3 This article shall be inoperative unless it shall have been ratified as an amendment to the Constitution by the legislatures of the several States, as provided in the Constitution, within seven years from the date of the submission hereof to the States by the Congress.

Article XIX*

The right of citizens of the United States to vote shall not be denied or abridged by the United States or by any State on account of sex.
The Congress shall have power to enforce this article by appropriate legislation.

Article XX†

SECTION 1 The term of the President and Vice President shall end at noon on the 20th day of January, and the terms of Senators and Representatives at noon on the 3rd day of January, of the years in which such terms would have ended if this article had not been ratified; and the terms of their successors shall then begin.

SECTION 2 The Congress shall assemble at least once in every year, and such meeting shall begin at noon on

* Adopted in 1920.
† Adopted in 1933.

the 3rd day of January, unless they shall by law appoint a different day.

SECTION 3   If, at the time fixed for the beginning of the term of the President, the President elect shall have died, the Vice President elect shall become President. If a President shall not have been chosen before the time fixed for the beginning of his term, or if the President elect shall have failed to qualify, then the Vice President elect shall act as President until a President shall have qualified; and the Congress may by law provide for the case wherein neither a President elect nor a Vice President elect shall have qualified, declaring who shall then act as President, or the manner in which one who is to act shall be selected, and such person shall act accordingly until a President or Vice President shall have qualified.

SECTION 4   The Congress may by law provide for the case of the death of any of the persons from whom the House of Representatives may choose a President whenever the right of choice shall have devolved upon them, and for the case of the death of any of the persons from whom the Senate may choose a Vice President whenever the right of choice shall have devolved upon them.

SECTION 5   Sections 1 and 2 shall take effect on the 15th day of October following the ratification of this article.

SECTION 6   This article shall be inoperative unless it shall have been ratified as an amendment to the Constitution by the legislatures of three fourths of the several States within seven years from the date of its submission.

Article XXI*

SECTION 1   The Eighteenth Article of Amendment to the Constitution of the United States is hereby repealed.

SECTION 2   The transportation or importation into any State, Territory or Possession of the United States for delivery or use therein of intoxicating liquors in violation of the laws thereof is hereby prohibited.

SECTION 3   This article shall be inoperative unless it shall have been ratified as an amendment to the Constitution by conventions in the several States, as provided in the Constitution, within seven years from the date of submission hereof to the States by the Congress.

Article XXII†

SECTION 1   No person shall be elected to the office of the President more than twice, and no person who has held the office of President, or acted as President, for more than two years of a term to which some other person was elected President shall be elected to the office of the President more than once. But this Article shall not apply to any person holding the office of President when this Article was proposed by Congress, and shall not prevent any person who may be holding the office of President, or acting as President, during the term within which the Article becomes operative from holding the office of President or acting as President during the remainder of such term.

* Adopted in 1933.
† Adopted in 1951.

SECTION 2 This article shall be inoperative unless it shall have been ratified as an amendment to the Constitution by the legislatures of three-fourths of the several States within seven years from the date of its submission to the States by the Congress.

Article XXIII*

SECTION 1 The District constituting the seat of Government of the United States shall appoint in such manner as the Congress may direct:

A number of electors of President and Vice President equal to the whole number of Senators and Representatives in Congress to which the District would be entitled if it were a State, but in no event more than the least populous State; they shall be in addition to those appointed by the States, but they shall be considered, for the purpose of the election of President and Vice President, to be electors appointed by a State; and they shall meet in the District and perform such duties as provided by the twelfth article of amendment.

SECTION 2 The Congress shall have power to enforce this article by appropriate legislation.

Article XXIV†

SECTION 1 The right of citizens of the United States to vote in any primary or other election for President or Vice President, for electors for President or Vice President, or for Senator or Representative in Congress, shall not be denied or abridged by the United

* Adopted in 1961.
† Adopted in 1964.

States or any State by reason of failure to pay any poll tax or other tax.

SECTION 2   The Congress shall have power to enforce this article by appropriate legislation.

Article XXV*

SECTION 1   In case of the removal of the President from office or his death or resignation, the Vice President shall become President.

SECTION 2   Whenever there is a vacancy in the office of the Vice President, the President shall nominate a Vice President who shall take the Office upon confirmation by a majority vote of both houses of Congress.

SECTION 3   Whenever the President transmits to the President pro tempore of the Senate and the Speaker of the House of Representatives his written declaration that he is unable to discharge the powers and duties of his office, and until he transmits to them a written declaration to the contrary, such powers and duties shall be discharged by the Vice President as Acting President.

SECTION 4   Whenever the Vice President and a majority of either the principal officers of the executive departments, or of such other body as Congress may by law provide, transmit to the President pro tempore of the Senate and the Speaker of the House of Representatives their written declaration that the President is unable to discharge the powers and duties of his office, the Vice President shall immediately assume the powers and duties of the office as Acting President.

* Adopted in 1967.

Thereafter, when the President transmits to the President pro tempore of the Senate and the Speaker of the House of Representatives his written declaration that no inability exists, he shall resume the powers and duties of his office unless the Vice President and a majority of either the principal officers of the executive department, or of such other body as Congress may by law provide, transmit within four days to the President pro tempore of the Senate and the Speaker of the House of Representatives their written declaration that the President is unable to discharge the powers and duties of his office. Thereupon Congress shall decide the issue, assembling within 48 hours for that purpose if not in session. If the Congress, within 21 days after receipt of the latter written declaration, or, if Congress is not in session, within 21 days after Congress is required to assemble, determines by two-thirds vote of both houses that the President is unable to discharge the powers and duties of his office, the Vice President shall continue to discharge the same as Acting President; otherwise, the President shall resume the powers and duties of his office.

Article XXVI*

SECTION 1   The right of citizens of the United States, who are eighteen years of age, or older, to vote shall not be denied or abridged by the United States or by any state on account of age.

SECTION 2   The Congress shall have the power to enforce this article by appropriate legislation.

* Adopted in 1971.

Proposed Article XXVII

SECTION 1   Equality of rights under the law shall not be denied or abridged by the United States or by any state on account of sex.

SECTION 2   The Congress shall have the power to enforce, by appropriate legislation, the provisions of this article.

SECTION 3   This amendment shall take effect two years after the date of ratification.

Proposed to states for ratification 22 March 1972, with terminal date 22 March 1979. Extension of three years and three months granted 6 October 1978. Amendment failed of ratification 30 June 1982, and became dead as of that date.—J.A.M.

About the Author

JAMES MICHENER was born in 1907 and raised by a Quaker woman in Pennsylvania. During World War II he served with the U.S. Navy and traveled across the Pacific. His TALES OF THE SOUTH PACIFIC won the Pulitzer Prize in 1947. His latest novel ALASKA is being published by Random House in June 1988.

He currently lives in Coral Gables, Florida and teaches at the University of Miami.

Vitus Bering and James Cook, two of the grandest names in Alaskan history, had mournful ends, the first dying of scurvy on a bleak, treeless, wind-swept island at the age of sixty-one, his life and his work incomplete. The second, having conquered scurvy and the farthest oceans, died at fifty-one because of his own impetuousness on a beautiful tropical island far to the south. The oceans of the world were made more available by the explorations of such men.

But there were in these years another kind of explorer, adventurer, and in 1780 such a one wandered almost accidentally into Lapak Bay in a small, incredibly tough little ship called the *Evening Star*, a two-masted, square-rigged whaling brig out of Boston. It was captained by a small, wiry man as resolute morally as his ship was physically. He was Noah Pym, forty-one years old and already a veteran of the dreadful gales at Cape Horn, the trading marts at Canton, the lovely coastline of Hawaii, and all the vast empty spaces of the Pacific where whales might hide, for if his ship was not big, it was valiant, and in it Pym was ready to challenge any storm or any group of hostile natives gathered on a beach.

Unlike Bering and Cook, Pym never left port with support from his government or cheering notice from his fellow citizens. The most he could expect would be a one-line notice in the Boston newspaper: 'On this day the *Evening Star*, Noah Pym with crew of twenty-one, sailed for South Seas, intended stay six years.' And as for the great nations agreeing among themselves to give this tough little fellow free passage, they were far more likely to sink him on sight in the supposition that he was sailing for the enemy. Indeed, he had in his time fought off the warships of both France and England, but this was a misnomer, for what he really did was maintain a sharp lookout and run like a frightened demon at the first sight of a sail that might prove threatening.

Zagoskin and Innokenti were out in their two-man kayak chasing sea otters when the *Evening Star* hove into sight off the south shore of Lapak Island, and they were astounded when a voice from the aft deck called out in good Russian: 'Ho there! We need water and stores.'

'Who are you?' Innokenti called, establishing that he was in charge.

'Whaler *Evening Star*, Boston, Noah Pym commanding.'

Innokenti, surprised that a ship from that far distance should have found Lapak Island, shouted back: 'Good harbor on the north shore south of the volcano!' and with Zagoskin paddling strongly from the rear seat, he led the way.

When the ship anchored between the shore and the volcano, Innokenti and Zagoskin climbed aboard and satisfied themselves in two minutes that whereas the *Evening Star* did carry one gun fore, it was not a warship. Neither man had ever seen a whaler before, but under the tutelage of the sailor who had called to them in Russian, they quickly learned what the procedures were, and just as quickly saw that Captain Noah Pym out of Boston was, though small, a leathery individual with whom it would not be profitable to quarrel accidentally.

They learned that this amazing little brig which had traveled so far—Cape Horn, China, a try at Japan, Hawaii—had in its crew sailors who could speak most of the languages of the Pacific, so that wherever the ship anchored, someone could conduct business with the natives. Only one man spoke Russian, Seaman Atkins, but he loved to talk, and for two rewarding days he, Innokenti and Captain Pym traded information on the Pacific.

Pym, once the ice was broken, enjoyed the swift interchange: 'Six men in Boston own the *Evening Star* and they award me a full share for serving as their captain.'

'Do you also receive pay?' Innokenti asked.

'Small but regular. My real pay comes from my captain's share of the whale oil we deliver and the sale of goods we bring home from China.'

'Do the sailors share?'

'Like me, small pay, big rewards if we catch whales.' Pym pointed to a sturdy young fellow, a New Englander almost as hefty as Zagoskin and with the same kind of scowl: 'That's Kane, our harpooner. Very skilled. Gets double if he succeeds.'

'Why have you come into our waters?' Innokenti asked, and Harpooner Kane frowned at the word *our*, but Captain Pym answered courteously: 'Whales. They must be up there,' and he pointed toward the arctic.

Zagoskin broke in rudely: 'We see them coming past here sometimes,' and he would have said more had not Innokenti signaled that this was privileged information. The baldheaded Russian was obviously irritated by this tacit reprimand, and both Pym and Atkins caught the warning, but neither commented.

On the third day the men of the *Evening Star* met Trofim Zhdanko, now in his late seventies and still unbearded out of his respect for the memory of Tsar Peter, and they trusted him from the start, in contrast to their rejection of the two younger men. The old fellow, at last in the company of someone who could speak Russian, poured out his recollection of Captain Bering, that hard winter on Bering Island, and the remarkable accomplishments of the German scientist Georg Steller: 'He went to four universities and knew everything. He saved my life because he made this brew of weeds and things that cured scurvy.'

'Now what might that be?' Pym asked. He had the habit of staring hard at anyone with whom he was speaking on important subjects, his small eyes closing almost to beads, his close-cropped head of brown hair bent forward.

'Scurvy is what kills sailors.'

'I know that,' Pym said impatiently. 'But what was in the brew this Steller made?' Trofim did not know exactly: 'Weeds and kelp, that I remember. First time I tasted it I spit it out, but Steller told me, right over there it was, behind that group of rocks, he said: "You may not want it but your blood does," and later on, when we spent that dreadful winter on Bering Island, I looked forward to the little amount of brew he allowed me each day. It tasted far better than honey, for I could feel it rushing into my blood to keep me alive.'

'Do you still drink it?'

'No. Seal meat, especially blubber and guts, they're just as good. You eat seal you never have scurvy.'

'What will happen up here?' Pym asked. 'I mean Spain, England, France, maybe even China? Don't they all have an interest in this area?' And he pointed eastward to the unknown area which the Great Shaman Azazruk had once called Alaxsxaq, the Great Land.

'It's already Russian,' Trofim said without hesitation.

'I was with Captain Bering when he discovered it for the tsar.'

On the evening before departure Captain Pym broached with Zhdanko the navigational problem which had brought him to Lapak, and it was premonitory that he did not reveal his questions to either of the two Russian leaders, for he already distrusted them: 'Zhdanko, what do you know of the oceans north of here?'

Since it was obvious that Pym was toying with the idea of sailing north, a difficult adventure, as Zhdanko had learned from his own explorations beyond the Arctic Circle, the cossack felt he must warn the American: 'Very dangerous. Ice comes crashing down in winter.'

'But there must be whales up there.'

'There are. They swim past here all the time. Going, coming.'

'Has any small ship . . . like ours . . . sailed north?'

Since Zhdanko did not know where Captain Cook had sailed after leaving Lapak Island, two years earlier, he could honestly warn Pym: 'No. It would be too dangerous.'

Despite this advice, Pym was determined to probe the arctic seas before other whalers would dare to venture into those icy waters, and he remained firm in his desire to explore them, but he did not share with Zhdanko his plans, for he did not want the other Russians to know them.

Next morning, Pym allowed himself an uncharacteristic gesture: he embraced the old cossack, for he saw in his noble bearing and generosity in sharing his knowledge of the oceans a man in the true tradition of seafarer, and he felt renewed for having been in contact with him. Summoning Atkins, he said: 'Ask the old fellow why he lives alone in this little hut?' and when the question was put, Zhdanko shrugged, pointed to where his stepson and Zagoskin were whispering, and said with resignation and repugnance: 'Those two.'

AFTER PYM, WITH NO KNOWLEDGE OR CHARTS TO GUIDE him, sailed his *Evening Star* north from Lapak, he entered a world into which no other American had ventured or would soon do so. Yankee ships had penetrated the rest of the major oceans, following quietly in the more spectacular wake of Captain Cook's ships. But the constant search for whales, whose oil for lamps, ambergris for perfumery and baleen for the stays in women's corsets would produce fortunes for shipowners and their captains, made exploration of untapped seas obligatory. To go north of the Aleutians was daring, but if whales existed in the area, the risk was worth it, and Noah Pym was a man to take that risk.

He lived a hard life. He was a devoted father, but he was away on his voyages for years at a time, so that when he returned home he scarcely knew his three daughters. But the results were so profitable to all concerned in his expeditions that both his owners and his crew urged him to sail yet again, and he did much sooner than he would have on his own account. He kept a cadre of reliable hands with him—John Atkins who spoke both Chinese and Russian; Tom Kane, the expert harpooner without whom the ship would have been powerless when a whale was sighted; and Miles Corey, the first mate, who was a better navigator than Pym himself—and even in bad weather he slept easily knowing that these men and others like them were in charge. He suspected that Corey was a crypto-Catholic, but if so, he created no problems aboard ship.

With the Aleutians left far behind, the *Evening Star* entered upon those dangerous waters which seemed so congenial in early spring, so fearful in October and November, when ice could form overnight, or come crashing down of an afternoon, already formed into great icebergs farther north and now cruising free on their own. When Captain Cook had faced this emerging barrier in August of 1778, he took one look, remembered the towering ice fields he had seen in Antarctica, and fled, as any sagacious mariner should.

Noah Pym, in search of whales instead of knowledge, captured one whale south of that narrow strait where the continents seemed to meet, and having heard in Hawaii the rumor that Bering and Cook in their larger ships had proceeded farther north without incident, he decided to do the same. In the Arctic Ocean, Harpooner Kane struck a large whale, and when Pym laid his ship close to the dying beast, landing boards were laid to its carcass so that sailors could cut it up, searching for baleen and ambergris and throwing great slabs of blubber on the deck for reduction to oil in the smoking pots.

While the brig lay idle as the oil was rendered, Mr. Corey, in a voice that betrayed no panic, warned the captain: 'Should the ice start to move down upon us, we must be prepared to run.' Pym listened, but since he had no experience in such waters, he did not appreciate how swiftly the ice could strike. 'We must both watch it closely,' he said, but when the harpooner stabbed a second whale with a splendid shot, work on salvaging it became so exciting, with promise of full casks for the long sail home, that Pym forgot about the impending ice, and for several triumphant days attended only to the bringing aboard of baleen and blubber.

Then, like some giant menace looming out of a fevered dream, the ice in the arctic began to move south, not slowly like a wanderer, but in vast floes that made giant leaps in the course of a morning and stupendous ones overnight. When the floes appeared, almost out of nowhere, the free waters around them began to freeze, and it required only a few minutes for Captain Pym to realize that he must turn south immediately or run the risk of being pinned down for the entire winter. But when he started to give the order to hoist all sails, First Mate Corey said in a voice that still showed no emotion: 'Too late. Head for shore.'

The advice was sound, the only one that would enable the *Evening Star* to avoid being crushed by the oncoming ice, and with an adroitness that far abler navigators than they might not have been able to exercise, these two New England men used every breath of wind to shepherd their little whaler with its thrice-precious cargo toward the northern coastline of Alaska, and there at a spot almost seventy-one degrees north, later to be christened Desolation Point, they stumbled by sheer luck into an opening which led to a substantial bay, at whose southern end they found a snug harbor surrounded by low protecting hills. Here, shielded from pounding ice, they would spend the nine-month winter of 1780–81, and often during that interminable imprisonment the sailors would not curse Pym for his tardiness in leaving the arctic but praise him for having found 'the only spot on this Godforsaken shore where the ice can't crush us to kindling.'

They had barely started constructing a refuge ashore when Seaman Atkins, the one who spoke Russian, cried: 'Enemy approaching over the ice!' and with expressions of fear that could not be masked, the twenty other crewmen looked up from their work to see coming at them across the frozen bay a contingent of some two dozen short, dark-faced men swathed in heavy furs.

'Prepare for action!' Captain Pym said in low voice, but Atkins, who had a good view of the oncoming men, cried: 'They aren't armed!' and in the next tense moments the newcomers reached the Americans, stared in amazement at their white faces, and smiled.

In the days that followed, the Americans learned that these men lived a short distance to the north in a village of thirteen subterranean huts containing fifty-seven people, and to the vast relief of the whalers, they found that the villagers were peacefully inclined. They were Eskimos, lineal descendants of those adventurers who had followed Oogruk from Asia fourteen thousand years earlier. Seven hundred and twenty generations separated them from Oogruk, and in the course of time they had acquired the skills which enabled them to survive and even prosper north of the Arctic Circle, which lay nearly three hundred miles to the south.

The Americans were at first repelled by the meagerness of the lives these Eskimos lived and by the tight meanness of their underground huts roofed by whalebone covered with sealskin, but they quickly came to appreciate the clever ways in which the chunky little people adjusted to their inhospitable environment, and were dumfounded by the courage and ability the men exhibited in venturing forth upon the frozen ocean and wresting from it their livelihood. The sailors were further impressed when half a dozen men from the village helped them build a long hut from available items like whalebone, driftwood and animal skins. When it was completed, large enough to house all twenty-two Americans, the men had reasonably comfortable protection against the cold, which could drop to fifty degrees below zero. The sailors were awed when they saw how much these short men, rarely over five feet two, could shoulder when helping to carry the *Star*'s supplies ashore, and when all was in place the Americans settled down for the kind of winter they had known in New England—four months of snow and cold—and they were astounded when Atkins learned from sign language that they could expect to remain frozen in for nine months or perhaps ten. 'Good God!' one sailor moaned. 'We don't get out till next July?' And Atkins replied: 'That's what he seems to be saying, and he should know.'

The first indication of how ably these Eskimos utilized the frozen ocean came when one of the powerful younger men, Sopilak by name, if Atkins understood correctly, returned from a hunt with the news that a monstrous polar bear had been spotted on the ice some miles offshore. In a trice the Eskimos made themselves ready for a long chase, but they lingered until their women provided Captain Pym, whom they recognized as leader, Seaman Atkins, whom they had immediately liked, and husky Harpooner Kane with proper clothing to protect them from the ice and snow and wind. Dressed in the bulky furs of Eskimos, the three Americans started across the barren ice, whose jumbled forms made movement difficult. Such travel bore no relationship to ice travel in New England, where a pond froze in winter, or a placid river; this was primeval ice, born in the deeps of a salty ocean, thrown sky-high by sudden pressures, fractured by forces coming at it from all sides, a tortured, madly sculptured ice appearing in jagged shapes and interminably long swells that seemed to rise up from the depths. It was like nothing they had seen before or imagined: it was the ice of the arctic, explosive, crackling at night as it moved and twisted, violent in its capacity to destroy, and above all, constantly menacing in the gray haze, stretching forever.

It was upon this ice that the men of Desolation Point set forth to hunt their polar bear, but after a full day's search they found nothing, and night fell so quickly in these early days of October that the men warned the seamen that they would probably have to spend the night far out on the ice, with no assurance that they would ever find the bear. But just before darkness, Sopilak came plodding back on his snowshoes: 'Not far ahead!' and the hunters moved closer to their prey. But it was a canny bear, and before any of them had a chance to see it, the first of its breed any American would encounter in these waters, night fell and the hunters fanned out in a wide circle so as to be able to follow the bear should it elect to flee in the darkness.

Atkins, who stayed close to Sopilak and who seemed to be learning Eskimo words by the score, moved about to caution his mates: 'They warn us. The bear is dangerous. All white. Comes at you like a ghost. Do not run.

No chance to escape. Stand and fight and shout for the others.'

'Sounds dangerous,' Kane said, and Atkins replied: 'I think they were trying to tell me they expect to lose a man or two when tracking a polar bear.'

'Them, not me,' Kane said, and Atkins proposed that in the coming fight, the three Americans stay together: 'We have guns. We'd better be prepared to use them.'

The Americans and most of the Eskimos slept uneasily that night, but Sopilak did not sleep at all, for he had hunted polar bears before, with his father, and had been present when a great white beast, taller than two men when it reared on its hind legs, had crushed a hunter from Desolation with one smashing blow from its paw. It had driven the man right down against the ice and then torn at him with all four of its sets of claws. The man and all his clothing had been left in shreds, and that bear had not been taken.

There had been other hunts, some of them led by Sopilak himself, in which the monstrous beasts, more beautiful than a dream of white blizzards, had been tracked for days and brought to heel by wisdom and courage. Toward dawn Sopilak instructed Atkins: 'Tell your men to watch me,' and though the seaman tried to explain to the Eskimo that the Americans had guns, which would give them a sizable advantage if the fight did materialize, no matter how often in the darkness Atkins raised his arms and went 'Bang-bang!' Sopilak did not understand. He saw only that they had no clubs or spears, and he feared for their safety.

When a pale, silvery cold light broke, a scout far to the north signaled that he had the polar bear in sight, and none of the three Americans who experienced the next moments would ever forget them, for when they rounded a huge block of ice thrown high above the surface of the frozen sea on which they moved, they saw ahead of them one of the world's majestic creatures, as grand an animal as the mastodons and mammoths that had once crossed over to Alaska at this point. It was huge, so completely white that it blended with the snow, and agile with a lumbering grace that caused the human heart to hesitate, so overpowering was the sense of beauty and awkward energy the bear exhibited as it began to move away. A supreme example of animal majesty, it seemed to be at one with the ice sheet and with the frozen sky. A light snow that began to fall as day brightened enhanced the dreamlike quality of the hunt as Sopilak's men began their chase.

The polar bear, unique among its genus in color, size and speed, could easily outrun any one man, and it also had the capacity to dive headlong into those strange openings in the ice where water flowed free, swim vigorously to the other side, clamber with amazing ease onto the new ice, and scamper off to other frozen areas where the men could not pursue, since they could not cross the open water. But it could not outrun half a dozen pestering men, especially when with spears and clubs and wild shouting they prevented it from attaining open water. So the long day's fight was about equal: the men could harass it and keep it from open water; it could outrun them and swim short distances to new positions. But in the end their persistence and anticipation of its moves enabled them to stay close and to drive it so that it winded itself, and in this manner the fight continued.

But as day began to wane, and it was brief at this autumn latitude, the men realized that they must soon come to grips with the bear or run the risk of losing it in the long night. So two Eskimos, Sopilak and another, became much more daring, and in a pair of coordinated thrusts they ran at the bear, confused it, and with Sopilak's spear damaged his left hind leg, and when they saw that he was wounded, two other men dashed in from behind, evaded the deadly swipe of forepaws when it turned, and struck again, in the same leg.

The bear was now seriously wounded, and knew it, so it retreated until its back was against a large block of ice which protected it in that quarter, and now the men had to attack from positions where it could spot them from the moment they began to approach, and in this posture it was formidable, a towering white giant, red-bloodied in one leg but the possessor of claws that could rip out a man's guts.

In this moment of equal battle, when the Eskimo who first charged knew that he stood a strong likelihood of being disemboweled, none of Sopilak's hunters volunteered to make the possibly sacrificial run, so the master hunter knew that it devolved upon him. He succeeded in striking the bear's undamaged right leg, but in endeavoring to escape, he fell under the bear's full glare, and a mighty swing of the right paw sent him sprawling flat upon the ice and exposed to the bear's revenge.

In this extremity, two Eskimos darted bravely out to incapacitate the bear, regardless of what happened to Sopilak, but they were so tardy that the bear had time to leap at its fallen enemy and would have crushed him and torn him apart had not Captain Pym and Harpooner Kane discharged their rifles at this moment to stagger the great white monster. With two bullets in it, an experience never known before, the bear stopped and gasped, whereupon Atkins fired his gun, and this bullet lodged in the bear's head, causing it to lose control and to fall powerless across the prone body of the master hunter.

There the marvelous bear died, this creature of the frozen seas, this magnificent giant whose fur was often whiter than the snow upon which it moved, and when the seven Eskimos saw that it was truly dead they did something that amazed the three Americans: they began to dance, solemnly and with tears streaming down their faces, and the man holding wounded Sopilak erect so that he too could participate began to chant a song that reached back five thousand years, and there as darkness fell the men of Desolation wept and danced in honor of the great white creature they had killed. Seaman Atkins, watching this performance, appreciated its meaning instantly, and in response to some ancient force that his ancestors in Europe had revered, he dropped the gun which had been instrumental in killing the bear and joined the dancers, and Sopilak took his hand and welcomed him to the circle, and picking up the rhythm, Atkins joined the chant, for he too honored the splendid white bear, that creature of the north that had been so majestic in life, so brave in death.

SOPILAK HAD A FIFTEEN-YEAR-OLD SISTER NAMED Kiinak, and in the days following the kill of the polar bear she worked with her mother and the other women of Desolation in butchering and tending to the valuable bones, sinews and magnificent white skin. As she did so, she became aware that the young seaman from the *Evening Star* was placing himself near her, watching her. With the Eskimo words which he was acquiring so rapidly, he had been able to explain to Sopilak and his mother that he, Atkins, as one of the cooks aboard the American vessel, wanted to learn how the Eskimos handled the meat of the bear, the walrus and the seal that they caught in winter, and this explanation was accepted.

But the Eskimo men who had participated in the famous hunt of this bear also knew that it was only the bravery of Atkins and his leader, Noah Pym, that had saved the life of Sopilak, and since they had told the story of those culminating moments, the heroism of the young man was known throughout the village, and his attendance upon the butchering and Kiinak was accepted and even encouraged. Several times Sopilak told the villagers: 'The young one saved my life,' and whenever he said this, Kiinak smiled.

She was a lively person, just under five feet tall, broad-shouldered, broad-faced, with a smile that charmed all upon whom it fell. But her outstanding characteristic was a heavy head of very black hair, which she kept cut so low that it obscured her eyebrows and shook from side to side when she laughed, which she did many times each day, for she loved the great nonsense of the world: the pomposity of her brother when he killed a walrus or captured a seal, the posturing of some young woman trying to attract the attention of her brother, or even the whimpering behavior of a child who was trying to enforce his will upon his mother. When she talked, she had the habit of using her left hand in a wide, careless sweep to brush the hair out of her eyes, and at such times she seemed quite gamine, and the older women of the village knew very well that this girl Kiinak was going to give the young men of the village much to think about as the time came for her to select a husband.

There was one other charming aspect, which John Atkins noticed the first time he saw her in the hut she shared with Sopilak and his young wife: Kiinak was not, like many Eskimo women, heavily tattooed about the face, but she did have two parallel slim blue lines coming down from her lower lip to the edge of her chin, and they gave her rather large, square face a touch of delicacy, for when she smiled the lines seemed to participate, thus making her warm smile even more generous.

When the butchering of the bear was completed on the spot where it had been slain, and the hundreds of pounds of rich meat lugged ashore for treatment in various ways, Atkins had no utilitarian reason for lingering about Sopilak's hut, but he did, and it was not long before the gossipy women of Desolation began predicting that something of interest was going to happen one of these days. And now came an amusing contradiction, the kind that confused many societies: the older women were romantics who reveled in watching how young girls attracted and bewildered young men, and they spent many hours speculating on who was going to go to bed with whom and what kind of scandal this might produce; but they were also rigorous moralists and protectors of village continuity.

Through long centuries they had learned that Eskimo society functioned best when girls postponed having babies until they had fastened themselves to some reassuring man who would provide for their children. Widespread flirtation and even bedding down with this attractive young fellow or that was permitted and even encouraged—for example, if two aunts had an ungainly niece who looked as if she might never catch a man—but if that niece had a child without first having found a husband, these same aunts would excoriate her and even banish her from their hut. As one wise old woman said while watching the courtship of Seaman Atkins and Sopilak's sister: 'It's always better when things go orderly.'

The romantic half of their concern was quickly resolved, for although Atkins had returned to his long hut half a mile away when the butchering ended, he remained there only two days, after which he came plodding back to Desolation on snowshoes, longing to see his Eskimo lass. He arrived at noon, bringing with him four slices of bread as a present to Sopilak, his young wife, Sopilak's old mother and Kiinak. Tasting the strange food outside their hut so as to enjoy the final few hours of faint haze before winter clamped a perpetual frozen darkness over all, they asked Atkins: 'Is this what you told us about? Is this what white people eat?' and when he nodded, they said, not contemptuously: 'Seal blubber is much better. Fat to keep you warm in winter,' and Atkins laughed: 'We'll soon find out. Our bread is almost gone.'

And within the next week the Eskimos were starting to provide the marooned sailors with seal meat, which they learned to enjoy, and with seal blubber, the part of the animal that enabled the Eskimos to live in the arctic, which the white men could not force themselves to eat. And one afternoon, as John Atkins helped bring the meat to the ship, accompanied by Sopilak, who had caught the seal, he returned to the Point and lived thereafter in Sopilak's hut, sharing a sealskin bed with laughing Kiinak.

WHEN THE LAST DAYS OF NOVEMBER BROUGHT TOTAL darkness to the icebound ship, the twenty-one Americans living in the long hut—Atkins no longer being with them—settled into a routine which enabled them to withstand the terrible isolation. Most important, each day at what they judged to be high noon, Captain Pym attended by First Mate Corey marched to the rude ship's clock and ceremoniously wound it so that they could ensure having what they called Greenwich Time, which made it possible to calculate where they were in relation to London. The principle was simple, as Captain Pym always explained to each new sailor coming aboard his ship: 'If the clock shows it's five in the afternoon at the Prime Meridian in London, and our shot of the sun shows it's high noon here, obviously we're five hours west of London. Since each hour represents fifteen degrees of longitude, we know for certain that we're at seventy-five degrees west, which puts us in the Atlantic some miles east of Norfolk, Virginia.' Within a few years, wandering sea captains like Pym would have one of the new chronometers being perfected by English clockmaking geniuses, and with it they would be able to ascertain their longitude precisely; for the present, using the rough clocks available, they could only approximate. Latitude, of course, had been determinable with amazing accuracy for the last three thousand years: in daylight, shoot the noonday sun; at night, shoot the North Star. '159 degrees West Longitude,' Pym would chart each day as he completed winding, '70 degrees, thirty-three minutes North Latitude.' No other explorer had been so far north in these waters.

From the inadequate tables which mariners like Captain Pym carried with them, he calculated that at this latitude north the sun would quit the heavens sometime near the fifteenth of November and not reappear as even a sliver until sometime in late January. Harpooner Kane, hearing him speak of this, asked in a kind of stupor: 'You mean, no light at all for seventy days?' and Pym nodded.

But on the midday of November the sun was still faintly visible for a few minutes, low in the sky, and Pym heard Kane tell the others: 'Tomorrow it'll be gone,' but on the sixteenth it still lingered. However, two days later the merest edge of the sun appeared for two minutes, then disappeared, and the sailors battened down their minds and their emotions, going into the kind of hibernation which many of the other arctic animals followed.

They were surprised, however, by the discovery that even at this great distance north, a kind of magical glow did appear each midday, illuminating their frozen world for a few precious minutes, not with actual daylight but with something more precious: a wonderful silvery aura which reminded them that the loss of their sun was not going to be perpetual. Of course, when this ambient glow vanished, the ensuing twenty-two hours of pitch-black seemed more oppressive and the penetrating cold more devastating. But when things seemed at their worst, the aurora borealis appeared, flooding the night sky with colors the New England men had never imagined, and Seaman Atkins, on his casual returns to the long hut, informed them: 'The Eskimos say that the People Up There are holding festivity, chasing bears across the sky. Those are the lights of the hunters.' But when the temperature dropped to what Captain Pym estimated as less than seventy below, for even oil froze solid, the men ignored the lights and huddled by their driftwood fire.

234

A prudent captain, Pym insisted that his men rise from their beds at what would have been dawn if there had been a sun, and he wanted them to eat such food as they could assemble at stated meal hours. He asked Mr. Corey to maintain a watch around the clock, especially in the direction of Desolation Point, warning: 'Many ships in the Pacific have been taken by natives who appeared friendly.' He assigned tasks to keep his men occupied, and week by week he devised ways to make the long hut more habitable, but each afternoon, two hours after lunch, he and Corey and Kane hiked across the ice to check upon the status of the *Evening Star*. Each day they inspected the planking to see if ice pressures had broken the stout body of the ship, and they saw with relief that the sides were so properly sloped that the crushing ice found nothing solid to press against. When it did move in with such tremendous force that it would have destroyed any ship not carefully built or whose sides provided some protrusion against which to press, it found only the curved flanks of the *Evening Star*, and when it pressed against them it lifted the ship gently aloft, until the keel stood some two feet above the surface of where the unfrozen water would have been. The ship had been lifted right into the air, and there it stayed as if it were some magic vessel in a dark gray dream.

'She's still firm,' Captain Pym reported each afternoon as the inspectors returned.

But the solemn moment came at what would have been sunset, local time, when in the blackness of perpetual night Noah Pym gathered his sailors and by a whale-oil light conducted evening services:

'Oh, God! We thank Thee that our ship is safe through one more day. We thank Thee for the minutes of near-light at midday. We thank Thee for the food that reaches us from Thy sea. And we ask

Thee to watch over our wives and children and mothers and fathers back in Boston. We are in Thy hands, and in the dark night we place our bodies and our immortal souls in Thy care.'

After such a prayer, delivered with surprising variation as he invited God's attention to their daily problems, he asked each of his sailors in turn, those who could read, to take the Bible which accompanied him on all his trips, and read some personally chosen selection, and rarely did the soaring words of this Book resound with more meaning than there in the long hut beside the Arctic Ocean as the sailors read the familiar verses they had learned as boys in distant New England. One night, when it was Tom Kane's turn to read, this normally violent man chose from Acts a selection of verses that seemed to speak directly to their marooning and their encounter with the Eskimos:

'"But not long after there arose against it a tempestuous wind ... And when the ship was caught, and could not bear up into the wind, we let her drive. And running under a certain island ... we had much work to come by the boat ... when the fourteenth night was come, as we were driven up and down ... about midnight the shipmen deemed that they drew near to some country ... Then fearing lest we should have fallen upon rocks, they cast four anchors out of the stern and wished for the day ...

'"And when it was day, they knew not the land: but they discovered a certain creek with a shore, into which they were minded, if it were possible, to thrust in the ship ... And falling into a place where two seas met, they ran the ship aground ... And so it came to pass, that they escaped all safe to land.

'"And when they were escaped ... the barbarous people showed us no little kindness: for they kin-

dled a fire, and received us every one, because of
the present rain, and because of the cold."'

His constant remembering that he was still an officer of a
church back in Boston and that he was, in a very real
sense, responsible for the moral welfare of his sailors,
often placed Captain Pym in difficult situations, as when
he put his whaler into some island port and his men ran
wild with the tempting girls who came at them skimming
over the water on boards with flowers in their hair. Not
being unnecessarily prudish, he looked aside while his
men reveled, then reminded them of their perpetual
duties when he had them back at sea attending his evening prayers. He also knew that they would raise hell
when they hit ports like the one serving Canton, and he
told himself: Stay clear. Let the Chinese bash heads.

But his magnanimity ended where marriage or its
local equivalent was concerned, and when he saw how
deeply Seaman Atkins was involved with Sopilak's sister, he realized that he could not ignore the moral problems which could result, and one morning in December
when no hunting for seals was under way, he walked on
self-made snowshoes to Desolation Point, where he
sought the hut occupied by Sopilak, and once inside, he
asked to meet with Atkins and the girl with whom he was
living, but three others concerned in these matters insisted upon attending also: Sopilak, his mother and his
young wife, Nikaluk. Seated in a circle on the floor,
Captain Pym started his discussion of the timeless problems involving men and women.

'Atkins, God does not look with favor at young men
who live with young women in an unmarried state—to
the eventual detriment of those young women when the
ship sails and they are left behind.'

Now developed a bizarre situation in which young
Atkins, as the interpreter in the group, was required to
repeat in Eskimo the castigation his captain had deliv-

ered, but the relations which had always existed between Noah Pym, one of the notable captains out of New England, with his men were such that Atkins felt obligated to translate honestly, and when he did, Sopilak's mother broke in vehemently: 'Yes, it is all right to make'—and here she used a gesture which could not be mistaken— 'but to leave a baby behind and no man to feed it, that is no good.'

For the better part of two hours these six people on the edge of the mighty ocean, whose frozen blocks cracked and snarled as they spoke, discussed a problem which had confused men and women since words were invented and families came into being for the nurturing and rearing of new generations. The contradictions were timeless; the obligations had not altered in fifty thousand years; and the solutions were as obvious now as they had been when Oogruk sought refuge in these parts fourteen thousand years ago after family problems on the far shore.

The climax of the discussion conducted in such an awkward manner and with so many participants came when it was revealed that John Atkins, from a little town outside Boston, a good Protestant and unmarried, was profoundly in love with the Eskimo girl Kiinak and she in turn was so lost in love for him that come midsummer she was going to have his child.

Interpreting of this last intelligence was not required, for when Kiinak pointed to her growing belly, her mother leaped from the ground, dashed to the door, and began shouting into the darkness: 'The bad one is going to have a baby and she has no man. Woe, woe, what is happening in the world?' Her cries attracted three other gossips her age, and now Sopilak's hut was filled with recrimination and noise and attacks against both the girl and her lover, and when the riot was sorted out, Captain Pym learned to his confusion that whereas it was completely wrong for Atkins to have got this fine young woman, fifteen years old, with child, it had been quite all right for them to have conducted all the steps leading up to that unfortunate development.

It was at the height of this complicated moral chaos that Pym first became conscious of the fact that Sopilak's wife was indulgently smiling at his confusion, as if to say: 'You and I are above this nonsense,' and he found himself blushing and awkwardly aware that they had formed a kind of partnership. Nikaluk was tall for an Eskimo, thinner than usual, and with an oval face unmarked as yet by tattoos. Her hair was jet-black and trimmed straight across her eyebrows, but she lacked the impishness of younger Kiinak, who had now moved close to Atkins as if to protect him from the condemnatory women who were shouting at him.

The impasse was settled when Atkins suddenly rose to announce in Eskimo that he wanted to marry Kiinak and that she had told him she wished to marry him. Now the four older women danced with glee, and embraced Atkins and told him what a fine man he was, with Captain Pym all the while standing aghast at this unexpected result his visit to Desolation Point had produced. But Nikaluk, still smiling condescendingly from the rear, made no attempt to quiet the confusion or give Pym any sign of reproof for the disturbance he and Atkins had created.

As the turbulent morning drew to a close, Pym told the crowd that he believed Atkins should return to the long hut with him and talk things over, and although the older women feared that this might be a device for preventing the promised marriage, they had to agree with Sopilak, who was the leader of their village, that it should be allowed, so after holding hands ardently with his young love, Seaman Atkins solemnly bound on the skis that Sopilak had made for him and followed his captain back to the long hut.

There Pym gathered the crew, informed them of what

had transpired in the village, and awaited their amazed responses, but just as Harpooner Kane was about to make a suggestion, Pym interrupted: 'Mr. Corey, I believe we have missed winding the clock,' and after the two men gravely attended to this ritual, Pym restated their position at the edge of the Arctic Ocean: '159 degrees West Longitude . . .'

IN THE PUBLIC MEETING TO DISCUSS THE POSSIBILITY that John Atkins might have to marry his Eskimo girl, the first alternative voiced was eminently practical: 'If she's pregnant, find some Eskimo to marry her. Give him an ax. They'll do anything for an ax,' and before Captain Pym could oppose such an immoral proposal, several other sailors pointed out how impossible it would be for a civilized man from Boston, and a good Christian, to take back with him a savage who had never heard of Jesus, and this sentiment was about to prevail when a surprise comment altered the whole course of the debate. Big Tom Kane growled: 'I know this girl and she'll make a damned sight better wife than that bitch I left in Boston.'

Several sailors whose minds were undecided happened to be looking at Captain Pym when these harsh words were spoken, and they saw him blanch, gasp, and then say quietly: 'Mr. Kane, we do not invite such comments in this ship.'

'We're not aboard ship now. We're free to speak our minds.'

Very quietly Captain Pym said: 'Mr. Corey, will you accompany me and Harpooner Kane in our investigation of the *Evening Star*? And you will come with us, Seaman Atkins.'

Across the ice the four men went, and once aboard their ship Captain Pym began the daily inspection as if nothing untoward had happened; they saw that the ice, still pressing in from the ocean, had as before struck the sloping sides of the ship and lifted her higher in the air rather than crushing her against the shore; the sides were tight; the caulking held; and when the thaw came she would sink back into the sea, ready for the trip to Hawaii.

But when the tour was completed, Pym said almost sadly: 'Mr. Kane, I was sore grieved by your intemperate outburst,' and before the big man could apologize, the captain added: 'We know of your tribulations in Boston and sympathize with you. But what shall we do about Atkins?'

Corey interrupted: 'What Tompkin said is true. She is a savage.'

Pym corrected him. 'In her own way she's as civilized as you or me. The way her brother catches bears and seals and walruses is as able as the way you and I catch whales.'

Corey, not silenced by this apt comparison, addressed his next remarks to Atkins: 'You could never take her to Boston. In Boston a dark savage like her would never be accepted.' And Atkins astonished the three men by saying rather innocently, as if he were in no way annoyed by this intrusion into his affairs: 'We wouldn't go to Boston. We'd leave ship in Hawaii. I liked what I saw there.' Before the men could respond, he nodded deferentially to the captain: 'Granting your permission, sir.'

There in the dark hold of the whaler, with the casks of valuable oil on all sides, Captain Pym considered this surprising development. Almost as if an act of God had descended upon his ship, he could in one sweep salvage his Christian conscience, help to save the soul of an Eskimo girl, and get rid of the consequences by putting the young couple ashore in Hawaii. On only few occasions in a navigator's life would he encounter an opportunity to do so many sensible things at one time and discharge the responsibilities of all concerned.

'You have my permission,' he said as ice pressed upon his ship and the timbers creaked.

Back in the long hut, he informed the crew that he would, as a captain legally entitled to do so, perform the wedding of his Seaman Atkins to the Eskimo lady, but he also pointed out that for the marriage to be acceptable, it would have to be conducted aboard his ship, for he was not entitled to act in that capacity elsewhere. And he then skied to the village to deliver the same message, and when he made it clear to the intended bride, who now spoke a bit of English, that a celebration was to be held to which the entire village would be invited, she ran through the huts, shouting: 'Everybody come!' and when she returned to where Captain Pym waited she kissed him warmly, as Atkins had taught her to do. Astounded by her boldness, Pym blushed furiously, and then he saw young Nikaluk smiling once again.

That wedding aboard the creaking *Evening Star* was one of the gentlest affairs in the long history of the white man's contact with the Eskimo. The Boston sailors decorated the ship with whatever bits of ornament they could construct, and that was not much: a scrimshaw here and there, a doll of stuffed sealskin, a striking block of ice carved with hammer and chisel by a carpenter, showing a polar bear rearing on its hind legs. When the Eskimos caught on to the idea of decorating the empty ship, they were far more inventive than the sailors, for they brought across the ice ivory carvings, things made of entire walrus tusks and the most wonderful items woven and constructed from baleen, until Captain Pym, comparing what they had done with what the Americans had accomplished, asked First Mate Corey: 'Now who is civilized?' and the dubious Irishman answered cogently: 'Taken together, what they've brought wouldn't signify in Boston.'

The service that Captain Pym conducted was a solemn affair, outlined in pages printed at the rear of his

Bible, and it was made doubly relevant by a passage which he arbitrarily quoted from Proverbs:

'"There be three things which are too wonderful for me, yea, four which I know not: the way of an eagle in the air; the way of a serpent upon a rock; the way of a ship in the midst of the sea; and the way of a man with a maid."

'During this voyage we have seen eagles in the air and serpents on land. The way our ship escaped ice in the sea was truly mysterious, and which of us can understand the passion which has impelled our man John Atkins to take as his bride this lovely maid Kiinak?'

The ceremony made a profound impression on the Eskimos, for although they understood nothing of its religious significance, they could see that Pym took it with such high seriousness that this must be a true marriage. At its conclusion the older women attending Kiinak began to chant ritual words reserved for such occasions, and for a few precious moments there in the darkness of the *Evening Star* the two cultures met in a harmony that would not often be repeated in years to come, and never exceeded.

But of all the persons participating in this occasion and in the limited feast which followed, only pregnant Kiinak detected a collateral event which was going to have even greater significance, for as she watched the women during the feasting she observed her sister-in-law, and she whispered to her new husband: 'Look at Nikaluk! She's in love with your captain.'

And as the long, dark winter drew to a close, and the sun returned to the heavens, no more than a silvery shadow at first, peeking its head above the horizon for a few minutes, shivering and running away, Nikaluk was powerless to hide the abiding affection she felt for this strange man, so different from her husband, the notable hunter Sopilak. She was loyal to her husband and reverenced his skill in leading the villagers and keeping them provided with food, but she also recognized in Captain Pym a man of deep emotion and responsibility, one in touch with the spirits who ruled the earth and the seas. She observed how his men respected him and how it was he who made decisions and said the important words. More even than her admiration for his qualities was the fact that she thrilled to his presence, as if she knew that he was bringing to this lonely village at the edge of the icebound ocean a message from another world, one which she could not begin to visualize but which she knew intuitively must have aspects of great power and goodness. She had known two men from this world, Atkins, who had loved her husband's sister, and Captain Pym, who controlled the ship, and they were in their way as fine as her husband.

But there was also the fact that she was captivated by the idea of Pym, by the possibility that she might lie with him as Atkins had done so easily with Kiinak and with such joyous results. Driven by these impulses, she began to frequent the places where Pym would be, and she became the object of gossip in the village, and even the sailors in the long hut knew that their married captain, the one who took the Bible so seriously and had three daughters in Boston, had caused an Eskimo woman to fall in love with him, and she with a husband of her own.

Pym, an austere man who took life seriously, thrashed about in a blizzard of moral confusion: sometimes he refused to acknowledge that Nikaluk was in love with him; later, when he did confess to himself that complications threatened, he assumed no responsibility for them. In either case, he made not the slightest gesture toward Nikaluk, not even so much as giving her a glance, for he was absorbed in what he deemed a much more serious problem. 'When,' he asked his officers at New Year's, 'can we expect the ice to melt?' and one of them who had read books written by Europeans about Greenland gave it as his judgment that the ice would not start to melt until May, but when Atkins asked among his wife's people, they gave an appalling date which translated into early July, and when Pym himself consulted with Sopilak, he was satisfied that this later date was probably correct.

Only then did despair settle upon the men of the *Evening Star*, for in autumn when the ice trapped them they had accepted their imprisonment, expecting it to last till the end of March, when spring thawed New England ponds. And at the onset of winter they were almost eager to see if they had the fortitude to withstand its historic blasts and were proud when they did. But now to greet a new year and to realize that summer would be more than six months distant was intolerable, and frictions developed.

Some wanted to shift their quarters to the ship, but the Eskimos warned vigorously against this: 'When ice melts, strange things happen. Maybe worst time.' So Captain Pym ordered them to remain ashore, and each day his inspections were more careful. He was considerate in dealing with men who gave trouble, assuring them that while he understood their anxieties, he could not tolerate even the slightest show of insubordination.

He was pleased, therefore, when the Eskimos organized hunting trips far out on the ice, which still showed no signs of melting, for then his more adventurous men could accompany them to share the dangers. He himself went once to where a long lead of open water had lured sea lions north, and he had shared in the dangerous task of killing two and then lugging them home over the ice. 'If we keep busy,' he told the men and himself, 'the day will come when we'll break free.'

As the day Captain Pym calculated to be the twenty-fourth of January approached, he encouraged his crew by telling them that the sun, still hiding beneath the horizon, would soon be returning to the northern hemisphere, and at a speed that would make the noonday twilight grow longer and brighter. And he explained to those sailors who knew no astronomy: 'Yes, the sun is heading north, and it will keep coming till it stands directly over the Arctic Circle. Then daylight will last twenty-four hours.'

'Tell it to hurry up,' one of the sailors said, and Pym replied: 'As with all things ordained by God, like the planting of corn and the return of geese, the sun must follow the schedule He gave it.' But then he added a curious bit of information: 'The ancient Druids, who did not know God, expressed their joy at the sun's responsible behavior with prayer and song, and since the Eskimos are also primitive people, I suppose we can expect the same.'

But he was not prepared for the things that happened at Desolation Point, for when on the twenty-third of January the sun threw unmistakable signals that on the next noon it would show its face, the villagers went wild, and children cried: 'The sun is coming back!' Drums were produced and tambours made of sealskin fastened to rims of driftwood, but what seemed to be the focus of attention and delight was a huge blanket woven years ago from precious fur spindled into thread and woven into a stout cloth. It was colored with dyes gathered along the shore in summer and from the exudations of sealskin and walrus.

That afternoon Sopilak and two other men in ceremonial gear came solemnly on their skis to the long hut to announce that on the morrow, at high noon when the sun would reappear, the sailors were invited to its celebration, and gravely they bowed as Captain Pym had done when conducting the wedding in his ship. First Mate Corey, speaking for the crew, promised they would be there, but when the Eskimos had gone he said, not spitefully but with a certain cynicism: 'Let's see what these savages are up to,' and half an hour before noon on the twenty-fourth he and Captain Pym led their entire complement of sailors over the frozen snow to Desolation Point.

In the silvery darkness they joined a solemn crowd, a group of people who had lived for many months without sunlight, and there was muffled excitement as the Eskimos looked to the east where the sun had regularly reappeared in years past, a hesitant disk bringing rejuvenation to the world. When the first delicate rays flickered briefly and a gray light suffused the sky, men began to whisper and then cry out in uncontrolled joy as shoots of flame came forth, heralding the true dawn. Watchers from the dark huts gasped, and even the sailors felt a surge of joy when it became apparent that the sun really was going to appear, for they had resented this strange dark winter even more than the Eskimos, and as the villagers gazed in awe when the sun itself peeked over the edge of the world to see how the frozen areas had sustained themselves during its absence, a woman began to chant, and one of Pym's sailors shouted: 'Jesus Christ! I thought it would never come back!'

Then, in the brief moments of that glorious day when hope was restored and men were assured that the world would move as it always had, at least for one more year, people began to cheer and sing and embrace, with the sailors jigging in heavy boots with old women in parkas who had not expected ever to dance again with a young man. And there were tears.

But now things happened that the sailors could not have imagined and which, perhaps, had never before happened at Desolation Point, unpremeditated acts which captured the essence of this glorious moment when life began anew. Along the beach, where great blocks of ice protruded like the backdrop to some drama enacted by the gods of the north, a group of girls, eight

247

or nine years old, danced, and their little feet, clad in huge fur-lined moccasins, moved so gracefully as their bodies, smothered in furs, bent in unusual directions, that the sailors fell silent, thinking of their daughters or little sisters whom they had not seen for years.

On and on the dancing of the little girls continued, elfin spirits paying respect to the frozen sea, big feet clomping handsomely in the snow as they followed steps which had graced this day and this seashore for ten thousand years. It was a moment in time that would be frozen in the memory of all the Americans who saw it, and two big sailors, overcome by the sudden beauty of the spectacle, remained in the background but in their own clumsy way aped the movements of the little girls, and old women clapped, remembering those years long ago when they had greeted the returning sun with similar dancing.

But no one watching these little girls reacted so strangely as Captain Pym, for as he followed their unaffected steps and saw the joy with which they smiled at the sun, he thought of his own three daughters and unprecedented judgments came to his lips: 'My daughters never showed such joy in their lives. In our home there was little dancing.' Tears came to his eyes, a symbol of his confusion, and he kept staring at the dance; he could not join it as his sailors did, but he understood its significance.

While the sun was still visible on its brief stop to say hello, excitement grew among the huts, where Eskimo men busied themselves with something that Captain Pym could not see, and after a few moments all the Eskimos cheered as Sopilak and his fellow hunters, mature men all, brought forth the big blanket which Pym had seen earlier but whose purpose he had been unable to guess. Laughter and excitement attended its passage to the spot where the girls had been dancing, but still none of the Americans could fathom why a mere blanket should be causing such a flurry. But then it was unfolded, and Pym saw that it had been made in the form of a circle with a rim strengthened to provide handholds, which most of the men in the village now grabbed. At signals from Sopilak, they simultaneously pulled outward, causing the blanket to form the surface of a huge drum, which was instantly relaxed and as quickly drawn tight again. Under Sopilak's skilled timing, the blanket pulsed like a living membrane, now loose, now taut.

When the men indicated their confidence that they could operate the blanket, Sopilak paused, turned to the crowd, and pointed to a rather pretty girl of fifteen or sixteen with braided hair, a large labret in her lower lip and prominent tattoos across her face. Obviously proud to have been chosen, she jumped forward, flexed her knees, and allowed two men to toss her in the air and onto the waiting blanket, which had been drawn tight to receive her. As watching women cheered, the girl waved to assure them that she would not dishonor them, and Sopilak's men began to make the blanket pulse, lifting the girl higher and higher, but as she had promised the women, she deftly maintained her balance, remaining erect on her feet.

Then, suddenly, the men tightened the blanket furiously, all pulling outward at once, whereupon the girl was tossed high in the air, perhaps a dozen feet, and there she seemed to hang for a moment before falling back to the blanket, upon which she landed still upright on her feet. The villagers applauded and some sailors shouted, but the girl, surprised at how high she had been thrown that first time and knowing that much more was to follow, bit upon the upper edge of her labret and prepared for the next flight.

This time she soared aloft to a considerable height, but still she maintained her footing; however, on the final toss she went so high that gravity and a spinning motion acted upon her heavily padded body and she came down in a heap, collapsing with laughter as the men helped her descend from the blanket.

Kiinak, clutching her husband's hand, told him: 'None went higher than me, but that was last year,' and he, always aware of her pregnancy, said: 'That was last year.' However, after two more saucy girls went flying up toward the sky, Sopilak relinquished his place on the blanket and came to stand before his sister, saying: 'To make the baby strong,' and gravely she took his hand and accompanied him to the blanket.

'Wait!' Atkins shouted, terrified at the prospect of his gravid wife's flying through the air and landing on the taut blanket with a thump, but Kiinak held up her right hand, indicating that he must stop where he was. Agitated as never before, he watched as she was lifted onto the blanket and her brother resumed his place in the circle of men holding it.

Gently, as if dealing with a baby already born, they started the rhythm of the blanket, chanting as they did, and then at a nod from Sopilak they imparted just the right gentle lift, and the pregnant girl rose slightly into the air and was expertly caught as she descended, suffering no shock whatever from her brief flight. When she rejoined her husband, she whispered: 'To make the baby brave.'

A very old woman, one who had soared to the sky when young, was similarly honored, but the lift was too modest for her tastes. 'Higher!' she shouted, and Sopilak warned her: 'You asked us to,' and his men applied just enough pressure to send the old one well into the air, where miraculously she controlled her feet so that she landed upright. The sailors cheered.

And now it was the villagers who did so, because gravely Sopilak stepped before his wife and invited her to leap upon the blanket, which she did without assistance. For some years, when she was sixteen to nineteen, Nikaluk had been champion of the village, flying with a grace and to a height which no other girl could match, for it was not the men alone who determined how high a girl on the blanket would rise; the use of her half-bent knees and the thrust of her legs helped too, and Nikaluk was bolder than most, as if she hungered for the higher air.

The rhythm started. The blanket pulsed. The excitement intensified as Nikaluk prepared for her first leap, and the sailors leaned forward, for they had been told by Atkins: 'The champion. None higher.' However, both Nikaluk and the men working the blanket knew that on her first three or four tries she was not going to rise very high, because both she and they had to test strengths and calculate just when to snap the blanket with maximum power, timing it with the bending of her knees.

So the first four tosses were experimental, but even so the rare grace of this lithe young woman was apparent, and the sailors stopped talking to watch the elegant manner in which she handled arms, legs, torso and head during her ascension, and upon no observer did her lovely motion have a greater effect than upon Captain Pym, who stared at her floating in air as if he had never before seen her.

Then, with no warning, she shot skyward at a speed and to a height which left him astounded: 'Oh! Goodness!' More than twenty feet high above his head she hung motionless, every part of her body in delicate alignment, as if she were a renowned dancer in a Paris ballet, a creature of extreme beauty and grace. And now slowly, then gathering speed, she started downward in a posture that looked as if she would have to land awkwardly, but at the last moment she established control and landed on her feet in the middle of the blanket, smiling to no one and preparing herself and her knees for the next flight, which she knew would carry her even higher.

Coordinating with unspoken signals from her husband, she flexed her knees, took a deep breath, and soared into the air like a bird seeking new altitudes, and as she sped aloft, Captain Pym noticed a strange aspect of her flight: Those big fur boots she wears, her heavy clothing, they seem to make her more graceful, not less, and her control doubly impressive. She was a wonderful flying young woman, and there were not on the entire earth at that moment more than a dozen women, regardless of race, who could have equaled her performance and none who could excel. High in the air, with the sun about to bid her farewell, she hung at the apex of her art and she knew it.

On the last upward thrust of the blanket, she went higher than ever before in her life, and this was not because her husband pulled the blanket especially strongly but rather because she synchronized her whole body in one supreme effort, and she did this solely because she wanted to enchant Captain Pym, whom she knew to be staring at her, mouth agape. She succeeded in making a lovely arc through the sky against the quickly settling sun, and as she returned to earth like a tired bird, she smiled for the first time that morning and looked boldly at her captain in a gesture of triumph. She had been aloft where no woman of that village had ever been before; she had been one with the newly born sun and the great ice field whose days were limited, now that her earth was moving into warmth. And when she was lifted from the blanket she experienced such a surge of victory that she went not to her husband but to Noah Pym, taking him by the hand and leading him away.

THE CELEBRATION OF THE SUN LASTED TWENTY-FOUR hours, and three events in the course of that celebration became part of the tradition of the village of Desolation Point, some treasured, some better forgotten. The young woman Nikaluk went with the Boston captain Noah Pym to a hut where they made love throughout the night. The rough sailor Harry Tompkin from a seafront village near Boston crept down into the bowels of the *Evening Star* to tap a keg of Jamaica rum which had been stowed aboard for medicinal and other emergencies. With the dark, delicious fluid he and two of his mates got drunk, but what was more significant in the history of Alaska, in their generosity and general mood of celebration, they shared their alcohol with Sopilak, who was staggered physically and emotionally by its stupendous effect. And when the sun came up for a second dawning, certifying that its return was legitimate, the old women of Desolation gave Captain Pym a present which in time would strangle him in a remorse that would never dissipate.

The lovemaking was a beautiful experience, a splendid Eskimo woman, pride of her village, striving to understand what the coming of this ship to her shore signified, sought to hold on to such meaning as she could discern. She knew that Noah Pym was the finest man she would encounter in this brief life, and since she had for three months longed to be with him, she had deemed it proper to make her desires known at the celebration of the sun where she performed her ultimate act of reverence, the faultless leap to heights never attained before.

Her boldness in leading him to the twilight hut was not surprising in this Eskimo village, for although the older women disciplined the younger, forcing them to marry in an orderly way so that their babies could be protected and reared in security, no one assumed that marriage ended the desires of people, and it was not unusual for a young wife or husband to behave as Nikaluk had done; no stigma attached to it and life went on after such an affair pretty much as it did before, with no one the worse because of it.

But since sailors like those from the *Evening Star* went home from Eskimo land averring that 'this here husband offered our captain his wife, as hospitality, you might say,' the legend grew that the proffering of a wife to a traveler was Eskimo custom. It was not. About the same amount of affection between traveler and local wife developed at Desolation Point as in a rural community outside Madrid or one close to Paris, or London, or New York. Nikaluk the Eskimo sky-dancer from Desolation had sisters all over the world, and many of the good things that happened in the world did so because of the desire of these strong-minded women to know of the world before the world left them or they it.

But Sopilak's disastrous introduction to rum was not a universal experience. White men had distilled this drink, so exhilarating, so liberating, for many decades and they had introduced it to people all over the world, and Spaniards or Italians or Germans or American colonists could imbibe it moderately, celebrate immoderately, and be little affected next morning. But others, the men of Ireland and Russia, for example, or the Indians of Illinois, or the Tahitians whom Captain Cook respected so highly when they were not drunk, and especially the Eskimos, Aleuts and Athapascans of Alaska, could not accept alcohol one day and leave it the next. And when they drank, it did terrible things to them. On the morning that Sopilak, the great hunter, accepted the liquor from the unwitting Harry Tompkins, the long decline of Desolation Point began.

When Sopilak swished that first taste of rum about his mouth he considered it too biting and too strong, but after he swallowed it and felt its effect all the way down to the depths of his stomach, he wanted another sample, and with its warmth began that indescribable swirl of dreams and visions and illusions of endless power. It was a magical drink, that he realized in those earliest moments, and he craved more and then more. As spring returned he became the prototype of those myriad Alaskans who in later days became addicted to alcohol, prowling the beaches and waiting for the arrival of the next whaler out of Boston. They had learned that such ships brought rum, and no finer gift in the world existed than that.

It was a filthy business the good Christians of Boston were engaged in, Captain Pym's brother and uncle among them: fabrics to hungry buyers in the West Indies, slaves to Virginia, rum out to the natives of Hawaii and Alaska, and whale oil back to Boston. Unquestionable wealth was created, but the slaves, the whales and the Eskimos of Desolation Point were destroyed.

The present that the old women of the village gave Captain Pym was delivered on the second morning after he had with a remorse never experienced before left the hut of love and taken Nikaluk to her own, where he found her husband lying in a drunken stupor on the ground. In that awful moment he saw two old women pointing at him and Sopilak, and he could deduce that they were praising him for having done something miraculous to the fallen man so that he could enjoy his wife. They were criticizing neither Pym nor Sopilak; in a sense they were congratulating the former for a rather neat trick.

Then other women appeared bearing in their arms a garment on which they had been working for some time, and after they had raised Sopilak to his feet and slapped his face a couple of times, he took the garment from them, smiled sheepishly at the men who had gathered, and held out his arms to Captain Pym. John Atkins, who approved of all that was happening, translated:

'Honored Great Captain whose guns saved my life when we fought the bear, and who helped Tayuk and Oglowook to kill him when I could not, our village gives you this present. Your men have been good to us. We honor you.'

Bowing, he allowed the garment to fall free, and the sailors who were still celebrating fell silent as they saw the noble cloak which their captain was receiving. It was pure white, heavy, long: the fur of the polar bear taken on that early hunt.

Everyone insisted that he put it on, and he stood embarrassed and ashamed as Sopilak and Nikaluk draped the glorious cape about his undeserving shoulders. He wore it all the way back to the long hut and even during the inspection of the ship, but that night as the time approached for evening worship he laid it aside, and when the men looked to him for prayer, he turned ashen-faced to his first mate and said: 'Mr. Corey, will you offer prayer? I am unworthy.'

PYM'S SURRENDER OF EVENING PRAYERS TO OTHERS HAD a constructive aftermath, for when the trying days of late April arrived, with permanent daylight but no indication that the frozen sea would ever relinquish its stranglehold on the *Evening Star*, the sailors grew at first restless and then downright belligerent. Fistfights erupted for no reason, and even when they were halted by Corey's quick attention, a general surliness prevailed.

When it looked as if real trouble might erupt, one of the ship's quietest men came to Captain Pym with astonishing news: 'Captain, sir, I've found proof in the Bible that God knows our plight and has promised rescue.' When Pym gasped to think that the Lord should be concerned about this lost little ship and its sinful captain, the sailor asked shyly: 'I was wondering if I might read Scripture tonight?' and Pym had to say: 'That's no longer my province. You must ask Mr. Corey,' and when the young man did, Corey gave quick assent, for if anything promised to ease tensions, he would try it.

So after evening meal, with the light as bright as it had been at midday, this frail young man, his voice throbbing with emotion, read from an obscure passage in the often overlooked book of Zechariah:

256

'"Behold, the day of the Lord cometh, and thy spoil shall be divided in the midst of thee.

'"And it shall come to pass in that day, that the light shall not be clear, nor dark:

'"But it shall be one day which shall be known to the Lord, not day, nor night: but it shall come to pass, that at evening time it shall be light.

'"And the Lord shall be king over all the earth: in that day shall there be one Lord, and his name one.

Closing the Bible reverently, the sailor leaned forward to offer a brief emendation: 'Clearly, men, this prophecy pertains to us. When we sell our whale oil, the shares will be divided. When the ice melts, and it surely will, we shall be set free. Already we have continuous day, as the Lord ordained. And at evening time there is light, and the Lord our God does reign as king over all the earth. Since He has promised to save us, there is no need for bitterness now.'

Several sailors, grateful for what seemed like divine intervention, clapped hands as he finished, but Captain Pym, suspecting that he had outlawed himself from such dispensation, shivered and stared at his knuckles, but his remorse did not prevent him from spending hours and then days and finally nights with Nikaluk, so that when the ice did finally begin to melt, with the *Evening Star* slowly resuming her position as a ship floating in water, Nikaluk started asking the inevitable questions, using the patois which the sailors and their women had developed over the nine months of the marooning: 'Captain Pym, s'pose Atkins take Kiinak with him. Why not you?'

He told her frankly: 'You know I have a wife, children. You have a husband. Impossible.'

Without rancor, but with a realistic assessment of the situation, she said: 'Sopilak? He what you call drunk all time.' And she began insisting that Pym take her with him. She had no concept of either Hawaii, where Atkins was going, or Boston, where the others were headed, but she was confident and with good reason that she would fit in and find for herself and Noah an acceptable life, but for two conclusive reasons he found it impossible to consider taking her to Boston: I already have a family, and even if I didn't, I could never show her there. No one would understand.

He was nowhere near brave enough to share that second reason with her, especially since Atkins had had no hesitancy in marrying Kiinak, Boston or no, so he postponed telling her definitely that he would be leaving her behind when the ship sailed. Yet he could not break himself away from her, for he was ensnared in the great passion of his life, the one that awakened a man to what love and women and a life's destiny involved. She had already placed an imprint on his life that would never be erased, neither by time nor regret, and in a perverse way he found intense pleasure in strengthening the experience. He was in love with Nikaluk, and when he was away from her he could visualize her flying in the air, her heavy boots prepared for a sudden landing, her arms and hair outflung in a vision of wonder that few men ever had of their women. She was of the sky, and the ice, and the endless nights, and the quiet harmony of this village beside the Arctic Ocean. 'Oh, Nikaluk!' he sometimes cried aloud when he was alone. 'What will happen to us?'

He did not, like many American men who were in those days exploring the world and new societies, engage in sentimental reflection about the poor island girl left behind, as if she were going to cry her heart out while he went on to better things, unaware that she was going to handle the situation rather easily in her island paradise while he would be tormented about island memories in Philadelphia or Charleston. No, Pym saw Nikaluk as a human being equal to himself in all ways except the possibility of her living in Christian Boston. Mr. Corey had been right; she was, in so many respects that mattered, a savage.

But he continued to wear the polar-bear cloak and to luxuriate in its richness and the memories it held of those great days hunting on the ice. The long coat became his symbol as he moved about the *Evening Star* preparing her for sea. One morning Atkins brought his wife aboard, and when Captain Pym saw her, smiling and eager for adventure, his breath caught and he wished he were that young seaman bringing Nikaluk, so much more mature and lovely than Kiinak, aboard for the long voyage to the closing of his life.

The sun shone. The sea relaxed. The ice retreated, baffled for another summer but sullenly hoarding its strength for a swift return in autumn, and sails were set. All the people of Desolation came down through the mud to watch the departure, and it might have been a gala morning except that with the raising of the gangplank, this final severance from the shore that had treated the visitors so hospitably with seal blubber and dancing and loving women, Nikaluk ran from her husband, approached the departing ship, and wailed: 'Captain Pym!' Her husband ran after her, not to rebuke but to comfort, but he had that morning drunk the last of Harry Tompkin's rum, and before he could catch his wife he fell in the mud and lay there as the ship withdrew.

Land had scarcely been lost on the journey south to Lapak Island, where the whaler would replenish as best it could for the long run to Hawaii, when Captain Pym, on the bridge, suddenly called out: 'Mr. Corey, this polar bear is strangling me!' and with frantic hands he tore at the beautiful cloak, throwing it from him and kicking it into a corner when it fell.

When Harpooner Kane heard of the incident he went to the captain, saying: 'I too helped kill the bear. Can I have the cloak?' and Pym said hurriedly and with a sense of overpowering guilt: 'You are entitled to wear it, Mr. Kane. You have not covered it with shame.' And during the long, cold trip south to Lapak Island, Pym continued to refrain from reading the evening prayers, for he was indeed strangled: the bear, and Sopilak fallen in the mud, and Nikaluk flying magnificently in the air were all fragments of his agony, especially his memory of those little girls, so untouched by the coming of the *Evening Star*, dancing on the frozen beach to rejoice in the return of their sun.

THE ENFORCED STOP AT LAPAK ISLAND WAS BRIEF AND terrible. When the little brig entered the familiar water between the volcano and the island and saw the Aleuts in their kayaks and elegant hats, Harpooner Kane cried: 'Home port!' but they had barely anchored when the sight of Kane in that rich white cloak excited the two reprobates, Innokenti and baldheaded Zagoskin, to start whispering among their men: 'That ship out there must be crammed with furs,' and after two days of adroit spying, prolonged by dilatory action in delivering provisions to the ship, the talk became: 'Properly led, sixteen determined men could take that ship.' When this was secretly discussed among seven ringleaders, Innokenti reminded his fellows of something he had spotted when the *Evening Star* stopped at Lapak on its way north: 'Captain Cook had soldiers aboard his ship. This one has none.' And now the plotting began.

No one had yet made a specific proposal of piracy, but Innokenti, remembering how Captain Pym had relished talking with Trofim Zhdanko, encouraged the New Englander to spend time in the old cossack's hut, and this necessitated the presence of the interpreter, Seaman Atkins, who took his wife along. The sessions were protracted, and Trofim had an opportunity to see what an excellent wife the young American had acquired in the Eskimo girl Kiinak, and he became especially concerned about her pregnancy: 'How wonderful that one of the first Americans in these waters found himself an Eskimo girl that he wanted to marry...before a priest...like decent human beings.' He returned several times to this theme, finally betraying his deeper concern: 'How much better these islands would have been if men like my son had taken Aleut wives.' He smiled at the young couple and said: 'You're beginning a new race. May God bless you.'

There was a young boy named Kyril, son of a Russian brigand and an Aleut woman whom he had raped and later killed. When the Russian sailed off to an eastern island in the Aleut chain, he abandoned his son, who began to frequent Zhdanko's hut, where he helped the old man. Trofim was especially eager that Kyril see how easy and normal it was for a man like Atkins to marry an Eskimo woman like Kiinak: 'Let this be a lesson. Good lives come from good beginnings.'

'Are you married?' Captain Pym asked, and the old man said proudly: 'Most powerful woman in Siberia. She'd make a grand tsarina,' and he asked Pym: 'Have you a family?' and the captain flushed a deep red, giving no answer, but Trofim needed none; what the trouble was he could not guess, but that there was trouble he knew.

While these wandering conversations were under way in the hut, Innokenti and Zagoskin, defeated men in their advancing years who had accomplished nothing but destruction, were huddled with their fellow conspirators, coordinating their attack on the *Evening Star*: 'Tomorrow when the captain and the young couple go to talk with the old fool, you and you, keep them inside. Then Zagoskin and I, with you three, board the ship as if bringing them supplies. He goes below with one helper. I stay on deck with two. And all of you speed out in your kayaks. At this signal,' and he shouted in Russian, 'we take the ship.'

'And if they fight?' one of them asked.

'We kill as many as we have to.'

'The others?'

'Like the ones in the hut? We deal with them later. But get the ship, because then we can do almost anything.' It had been secretly agreed between Innokenti and Zagoskin that after capturing the ship, all survivors would be taken to nearby Adak and murdered, the blame being placed upon the Aleuts there.

The plot was uncomplicated and brutal, with an excellent chance for success, except that on the target day Captain Pym did not visit Trofim and Kyril; he stayed aboard ship and this meant that Atkins and his wife stayed too, but the conspirators were so sure of success that the plan went forward. At one in the afternoon the two leaders came to the *Evening Star*, accompanied by three traders, as agreed. They brought with them a substantial supply of stores, and as they began to deliver them, other men with more goods set out from shore.

Noah Pym, learned in the lore of ships' being taken by land-based natives, was below when the second contingent started to come aboard, and instinctively he rushed toward the door of his cabin, crying: 'Mr. Corey, what goes on?'

He was met by Zagoskin, who gave a loud bellow signaling that the fight had begun, and then clubbed Pym over the head, cracking his skull and knocking him to the deck. From that fallen position the dazed man raised himself on one elbow and tried to defend himself, but with a heavy boot Zagoskin kicked him in the face, whereupon Zagoskin's Siberian helper beat the little New Englander to death. He uttered no final words, entertained no last thoughts. He died trying to save his ship, which in his last moments he supposed he had lost. He was not even allowed time for prayer, which had been absent from his lips for so long.

Young Atkins and his wife, hearing the commotion in the captain's cabin, ran to his assistance, just in time to be clubbed to death by Zagoskin and his helper, who were then free to rush topside to help Innokenti clear the decks, but when they reached there they found far more confusion than they had anticipated, for First Mate Corey, an iron-tough Irishman, assumed that Pym was dead and that the salvation of the ship depended on him. Armed with pistol and sword, he killed two attackers and forced their leader Innokenti to stay back. But now, seeing huge Zagoskin coming at him, he shouted: 'Help! Help!' threw down his empty pistol and grabbed a belaying pin, determined to kill as many Russian pirates as possible before surrendering the ship.

At this moment a huge man in a long white cloak rushed on deck, wielding a long harpoon in each hand. It was Kane, shouting: 'Pym's dead. Kill them all!' And without stopping to take careful aim, he threw one of his lethal spears at the approaching Zagoskin. It sped through the air like a slim bolt of lightning, struck the Russian just above the heart and pinned him like a helpless seal to the mast.

Not satisfied that the harpoon had killed the man, Kane leaped at him as he stood speared and with his other harpoon stabbed him twice, once through the neck, once through the face. Then, failing to jerk the first harpoon loose, he abandoned it, grabbed the club with which Zagoskin had killed Atkins and his wife, and rampaged about the deck, striking with fury any Russians he encountered.

Joining with Corey, who was defending himself with only a belaying pin, Kane pointed to Innokenti and shouted to all the Americans within earshot: 'He's a bastard! Kill him!' and with that he launched his other harpoon at the instigator of the attack. He missed, and when Mr. Corey lunged at him, Innokenti deftly sidestepped and gained a moment to survey the deck where plans had gone so terribly wrong. He saw the dead Russians, his partner Zagoskin skewered against the mast, and both Kane and that damned Irishman summoning their men, so in one bloodstained second he made his decision. With a wild dive over the side he abandoned his cohorts and ignored the fact that he couldn't swim. With the superhuman power that evil men can often muster in the face of mounting disaster, this amazing scoundrel flopped about in the sea like a stricken fish, reached an empty kayak, upset it sideways, thrust his legs into one of the hatches, righted it, and with long skilled strokes fled toward shore. Corey, seeing him about to escape punishment, grabbed a pistol from a sailor and tried to shoot him, but missed. And after the Boston men had cleared their ship of invaders and tossed overboard the corpses of Zagoskin and his fellow pirates, Corey said in controlled voice, as if nothing of importance had happened: 'Up anchor, prepare sails. Mr. Kane, you are promoted to First Mate. Report to me on the condition of the crew.'

The last sight the Russian fur traders had of this doughty little ship—which had explored the seas, chased whales, and survived being pinned down in an arctic winter—was a file of men standing at attention along the port gunwales while the new captain read solemnly from a Bible, and a big man in a long white cloak lifted three bodies, one by one—Captain Pym, Seaman Atkins and the pregnant Eskimo girl Kiinak—and pitched them into the Bering Sea.

But that was not all, for when the ceremony ended, the new captain ordered the ship's ineffectual gun unlimbered, pointed ashore, and fired. A cannonball of no great weight ricocheted across the rocky land of Lapak Island, coming to harmless rest close to the hut occupied by Trofim Zhdanko, who had watched the events of this day with shame and horror.

*ALASKA by James A. Michener
is available at your local
bookstore, or use this coupon
to order by mail:*

*Turn the page to see if there's a Michener you've
missed . . .*

THE BRIDGES AT TOKO-RI

Young and innocent, arriving in a place they had barely heard of, they prepared for the ritual many men had endured before them—war. They were American fighter pilots, and they came on a huge ship that also carried their helicopters. Trained as professionals, but as frightened as every man before them who had ever gone to war, they would face an enemy they couldn't understand and wage a war they had to win.

CARAVANS

Ellen Jaspar's parents have not heard from her since her impetuous marriage to a young Afghan engineer. She was beautiful, daring, and bright. And fed up with being the pampered, obedient daughter of middle-class parents. Ellen wanted something more out of life than they could offer. She wanted to be free to do her thing. No one knew what that was. But it took her to a remote and primitive land and now it seemed that land had simply swallowed her up.

CENTENNIAL

The story of the land and its people—of Lame Beaver, the Arapaho chieftain and warrior, and his Comanche and Pawnee enemies; of Levi Zendt, fleeing with his child bride from the Amish country back in Pennsylvania; and of the cowboy Jim Lloyd, who falls in love with the wealthy and cultured Englishwoman, Charlotte Seccombe. It is a story of trappers, homesteaders, gold seekers, ranchers, hunters—all caught up in the dramatic events and violent conflicts that shaped the destiny of our legendary West.

CHESAPEAKE

The enthralling historical saga of our land and its people, focusing on the generations of seven brawling, burgeoning families—their failures and triumphs, their uniquely American spirit and drive—living on Maryland's Chesapeake Bay. "A magnificently written novel."   —Associated Press

THE COVENANT

The best and worst of two continents carve an empire out of the vast wilderness that is to become South Africa. From the Java-born Van Doorns spring two great branches of the family. One will create vast, lush vineyards. The other will settle the interior and become the first Trekboers and Afrikaners. From the Nxumalos, inhabitants of a peaceful village unchanged for centuries, come those who will unite warrior tribes into the powerful Zulu nation and intertwine forever with the Van Doorns. From the Saltwoods, wealthy spice merchants, come missionaries and settlers who join the masses and influence the wars and politics that will change a nation forever.

THE DRIFTERS

A poignant and powerful drama of six young runaways adrift in a world they have created out of dreams, drugs, and dedication to pleasure. Spun out against the exotic backdrops of Spain, Marrakech, and Moçambique, THE DRIFTERS reveals the frantic hedonistic pursuit of today's disenchanted youth. Michener pulls us to the dark center of their private world, exposing the naked nerve ends with shocking candor and infinite compassion.

THE FIRES OF SPRING

David Harper was an orphan. His legacy: loneliness and poverty. But his longing to embrace the world that abandoned him was stronger than the harsh realities. As an adolescent con man and petty thief at a carnival, David learned above love and about women. First with the vulnerable young prostitute, Nora, who gave him her heart as well as her body. Then with the others... all of whom taught him the riches of himself.

HAWAII

The #1 bestseller, the lusty saga of the Hawaiian islands, from its volcanic creation to the arrival of the white man. This magnificent chronicle of paradise, full of Michener's fascination with the Pacific, is an enchanting and mammoth biography of a people. "Exciting, lusty, vivid..."—*Chicago Tribune*

POLAND

Like the heroic land that is its subject, POLAND teams with vivid events and unforgettable characters spanning eight tumultuous centuries. In a tradition of resistance to barbarian Tartar invaders and brutal Nazi occupiers, with a heritage of pride that burns through eras of romantic passion and courageous solidarity, three powerful families live out their destinies—and the dream of a nation. Here are the Counts Lubonski of the nobility, the Bukowskis of the gentry, and the peasant Buks—at times fiercely united, at other times tragically divided—whose common story finds its breathtaking culmination in the historic showdown between implacable Communists and rebellious farmers in our present day.

RETURN TO PARADISE

Michener returns to the scenes from *Tales of the South Pacific*, which won him world recognition. Once again he evokes the magic of the blessed isles in the Pacific with stories and accounts glowing with color and alive with adventure. RETURN TO PARADISE is a new visit to a land of enchantment by one of the most gifted storytellers of our time.

SAYONARA

Major Lloyd Gruver considered himself a lucky man. Son of an Army general, he was stationed in beautiful, exotic Japan and was dating a general's daughter. His future looked pretty good. He couldn't understand guys like Private Joe Kelly. Marrying those Japanese girls, never being able to go back to the states. No, Gruver simply couldn't comprehend it. Then he met Hana-ogi. After that, nothing mattered anymore. Nothing but her...

THE SOURCE

The archeological dig at Makor uncovers artifacts that trace the history of Judaism, from the very beginnings of religion to the start of Christianity, through the Crusades, the Spanish Inquisition, up to the founding of Israel and the ever-present conflicts with the Arabs. The scientists at the dig, which is being financed by the wealthy American Paul Zodman, include Dr. John Cullinane, an Irish Catholic from Chicago, Jemail Tabari, an Israeli Arab, Ilan Eliav, a German Jew who lost his wife in the war, and Vered Bar-El, an Israeli woman who is engaged to Ilan and loved by John. Their discoveries from the past put new perspectives on the personal conflicts they must resolve.

SPACE

The arena stretching for billions of miles beyond the surface of earth. It is the object of dreams and daring of countless men and women who have made it the last great frontier of human endeavor. It is the setting for people like Stanley Mott, the engineer whose irrepressible drive for knowledge places him at the center of the American exploration effort. Norman Grant, war hero and U.S. senator who takes his personal battle not only to a nation, but to the heavens as well. Dieter Kolff, Hitler's rocket scientist who brings his precious specialty to an America on the brink of a new era. Randy Claggett, the lusty astronaut who meets his destiny on a mission to the far side of the moon. Debbie Dee Claggett, the astronaut's sensual wife whose marriage can never be as important as the space program. Cynthia Rhee, the glamorous reporter whose determined crusade brings the real truth of men among the stars to a breathless world.

TALES OF THE SOUTH PACIFIC

The exotic world of the South Pacific, with its endless ocean, the tiny specks of coral we call islands, the coconut palms, the waves breaking into spray against the reefs, the full moon rising behind the volcanoes, and the men and women caught up in the drama of the big war. The young Marine who falls madly in love with a beautiful Tonkinese girl. Nurse Nellie and her French planter, Emile De Becque. The soldiers, sailors, and nurses playing at war and waiting for love in a tropic paradise. Winner of the Pulitzer Prize.

TEXAS

A land of sprawling diversity and unparalleled richness, a dazzling chapter in the history of our nation, a place like no other on earth. The epic saga spanning four centuries and two continents, charting the dramatic formation of several great dynasties from the age of the conquistadors to the present day: the Rusks, who amassed a legendary fortune living by their own rules, the world be damned; the Quimpers, the quintessential Texas wheeler-dealers who lustily embodied the taller-than-life myth of their home state; the Cobbs, who parlayed an empire of cotton into unchallenged political wealth; the Garzas, a clan of peasants, bandits, and scholars, whose roots in the native soil lay deepest of all. The richly compelling novel of a proud people eager to meet the marvelous challenge of their land.

Nonfiction by James A. Michener

THE BRIDGE AT ANDAU

"The bridge at Andau was about the most inconsequential bridge in Europe...But by accident of history it became, for a few flaming weeks, one of the most important bridges in the world, for across its unsteady planks fled the soul of a nation." In Michener's words, this moving story of the Hungarian people's revolt against communism is a chilling drama of a nation's fight for survival and of the hunger for freedom that lives in the hearts of men and women all over the world.

IBERIA: Spanish Travels and Reflections

Spain is one of the most beautiful and fascinating countries on earth. And no one but James Michener could capture so brilliantly the essence, the richness, and the color of this wild, strange, and contradictory land. Here is an utterly unforgettable adventure by a writer whose gift for passionate observation is without equal.

KENT STATE: What Happened and Why

"There will probably never be a more thorough, minute-by-minute account than Michener's of the three days of disorder that preceded the shooting. Valuably, the book shows how easily divisions within a community can escalate toward tragedy. Michener convinces the reader when he says: 'Kent could be your community.'"—*Time* magazine

RASCALS IN PARADISE

Some craved power, some craved peace, others merely surrendered to fate. Sam Comstock—a sailor crazed by the South Sea Islands and driven to lead the ruthless mutiny. He envisioned himself a magnificent ruler—but his dream became a nightmare. Will Mariner—a golden-haired youth whose ship was captured by hostile natives. He was the sole survivor, and his charm turned his captors into slaves. Captain Bligh—was he the infamous captain of the *Bounty*, the monster legend had made him? Here is the true story. All of them searched for adventure in the most dazzling places on earth.

SPORTS IN AMERICA

There is a crisis in American sports, and it's getting worse. Pro basketball players are banned for narcotics use, while a major league pitcher is arrested for smuggling drugs across the Mexican border. An NFL quarterback is thrown to the ground and hurt after a play, while the league's "injury report" grows longer every Sunday. Corruption and recruiting violations plague collegiate sports, while the "winning is everything" mentality is espoused at the Little League level. Even before these problems made national headlines, James A. Michener was growing concerned over the state of sports. Out of his lifelong enthusiasm for sports comes this explosive, spectacular book.

To help commemorate the Year of the Reader, James Michener recently shared his thoughts on one of his favorite books.

THE BOOK THAT MADE A DIFFERENCE
by James A. Michener

In these words of wisdom about reading, there are really only two ideas worth clinging to. The first comes in the next paragraph. The second comes in the last. The intermediary stuff can be skipped.

A classic book is one that reaches you at the precise moment when it can make the most profound impression, that is, when you're ready for it.

In the very good college I attended, little Swarthmore in Pennsylvania, I had read by my junior year many of the fine books of preceding eras. Dostoevsky's *Idiot* was a splendid book. I was deeply moved by Butler's *The Way of All Flesh* and anything by Thomas Hardy concentrated my attention. But those, and a dozen like them made primarily an intellectual impact on me. They helped me answer probing questions on examinations and prove to my professors that I'd done the required reading and then some. I'm glad I read every one of them and profited from each.

But in the summer before my senior year I went on a boating trip to the Chesapeake, to which I would return almost fifty years later to write a novel growing out of the impressions I gained then, so the trip bore wonderful fruit.

But more important was the fact that I took along with me a copy of a novel about which I'd heard good reports but never had time to read. It was William Makepeace Thackeray's *Vanity Fair*, and I spent joyous days drifting down the Chesapeake and making the acquaintance of Becky Sharp and her perplexing and sometimes disreputable friends. How vividly I remember the dinner party in Brussels on the night before the Battle of Waterloo, and the movement in and out of London of the various important characters.

It was in following the intricacies of this novel that I first saw, in my own terms, how a work of fiction could be constructed. I saw the importance of setting, of character development, of the clever interposition of the author, of the value of witty observation.

In short, *Vanity Fair* was the first book I ever read as a novel, as a conscious construction for the purpose of enchanting the reader. I'd read most of Dickens and fine works like *Madame Bovary*, but not as prototypes of what the artist can do when he sets out consciously to engage his reader. Had I never read *Vanity Fair* at that period in my life, I might never have gained my understanding of what narrative really is. Later, in Arnold Bennett's *The Old Wives Tale* and in Thomas Mann's *Buddenbrooks* I discovered how to construct a narrative that covers more than one generation, and then I had my armament for the long battles ahead.

Had I not come upon these books when I did... No, let's say, had these great books not discovered me when I needed them, I'd never have become a writer. Today it's fashionable to denigrate Thackeray and when I last dipped into *Vanity Fair*, it creaked. No one reads Bennett anymore, but when I read him at the right moment he was explosive and I revere his memory.

One of the finest wishes I could make for any young person working on his or her education is that: "I hope you stumbled upon the right books when you're ready for them." Because if one doesn't, one runs the risk of never developing one's abilities. The right books can expand the mind, opening wholly new vistas, challenging possiblities.

The great truth of this closing paragraph must be obvious: "If you don't read widely when your lifetime values are forming, you may miss the book that could ennoble your life. They'll be cheering on the other side of the fence, but you won't be in the game."

James A. Michener's books are available in bookstores, or use this coupon to order by mail:

____ THE BRIDGE AT ANDAU	21050-2	$3.95
____ THE BRIDGES AT TOKO-RI	20651-3	2.95
____ CARAVANS	21380-3	5.95
____ CENTENNIAL	21419-2	5.95
____ CHESAPEAKE	21158-4	5.95
____ THE COVENANT	21420-6	5.95
____ THE DRIFTERS	21353-6	5.95
____ THE FIRES OF SPRING	21470-2	4.95
____ HAWAII	21335-8	5.95
____ IBERIA	20733-1	5.95
____ KENT STATE	20273-9	2.95
____ POLAND	20587-8	4.95
____ RASCALS IN PARADISE	21459-1	4.95
____ RETURN TO PARADISE	20650-5	3.95
____ SAYONARA	20414-6	2.95
____ THE SOURCE	21147-9	5.95
____ SPACE	20379-4	4.95
____ TALES OF THE SOUTH PACIFIC	20652-1	3.95
____ TEXAS (paperback)	21092-8	5.95
____ TEXAS (hardcover)	54154-5	21.95